Leo
24 July – 23 August

DID YOU PURCHASE THIS BOOK WITHOUT A COVER?

If you did, you should be aware it is **stolen property** as it was reported *unsold and destroyed* by a retailer. Neither the author nor the publisher has received any payment for this book.

All Rights Reserved including the right of reproduction in whole or in part in any form. This edition is published by arrangement with Harlequin Enterprises II B.V./S.à.r.l. The text of this publication or any part thereof may not be reproduced or transmitted in any form or by any means, electronic or mechanical, including photocopying, recording, storage in an information retrieval system, or otherwise, without the written permission of the publisher.

This book is sold subject to the condition that it shall not, by way of trade or otherwise, be lent, resold, hired out or otherwise circulated without the prior consent of the publisher in any form of binding or cover other than that in which it is published, and without a similar condition including this condition being imposed on the subsequent purchaser.

® and ™ are trademarks owned and used by the trademark owner and/or its licensee. Trademarks marked with ® are registered with the United Kingdom Patent Office and/or the Office for Harmonisation in the Internal Market and in other countries.

First published in Great Britain 2010
by Harlequin Mills & Boon Limited,
Eton House, 18-24 Paradise Road, Richmond, Surrey TW9 1SR

Copyright © Dadhichi Toth 2007, 2008, 2009, 2010 & 2011

ISBN: 978 0 263 87382 5

Typeset at Midland Typesetters Australia

Harlequin Mills & Boon policy is to use papers that are natural, renewable and recyclable products and made from wood grown in sustainable forests. The logging and manufacturing processes conform to the legal environmental regulations of the country of origin.

Printed and bound in Spain
by Litografia Rosés S.A., Barcelona

About Dadhichi

Dadhichi is one of Australia's foremost astrologers. He has the ability to draw from complex astrological theory to provide clear, easily understandable advice and insights for people who want to know what their future might hold.

In the 27 years that Dadhichi has been practising astrology, face reading and other esoteric studies, he has conducted over 9,500 consultations. His clients include celebrities, political and diplomatic figures, and media and corporate identities from all over the world.

Dadhichi's unique blend of astrology and face reading helps people fulfil their true potential. His extensive experience practising western astrology is complemented by his research into the theory and practice of eastern systems of astrology.

Dadhichi features in numerous newspapers and magazines and he also appears regularly on many of Australia's leading television and radio networks, where many of his political and world-wide forecasts have proved uncannily accurate.

His website www.astrology.com.au is now one of the top ten online Australian lifestyle sites and, in conjunction with www.facereader.com, www.soulconnector.com and www.psychjuice.com, they attract over half a million visitors monthly. The websites offer a wide variety of features, helpful information and personal services.

Dedicated to The Light of Intuition
Sri V. Krishnaswamy — mentor and friend
With thanks to Julie, Joram, Isaac and Janelle

Welcome from
Dadhichi

Dear Friend,

Welcome to your astrological forecast for 2011! I've spent considerable time preparing these insights for you. My goal is to give you an overview of your sign and I hope you can use my simple suggestions to steer you in the right direction.

I am often asked by my clients to help them understand their true path and what they are supposed to be doing in life. This is a complex task; however, astrology can assist with finding some answers. In this book I attempt to reveal those unique character traits that define who you are. With a greater self-understanding, you can effectively begin *to live who you are* rather than wondering about *what you should do*. Identity is the key!

Knowing when the best opportunities in your life are likely to appear is the other benefit of astrology, based on planetary transits and forecasting. The latter part of the book deals with what is *likely* to happen on a yearly, monthly and daily basis. By coupling this section with the last chapter, an effective planner, you can conduct your business, relationships and personal affairs in ways that yield maximum benefits for you.

Along with your self-knowledge, there are two other key attitudes you must carry with you: *trust* and *courage*. Unless you're prepared to take a gamble in life, earnestly and fearlessly, you'll stay stuck in the same place, never really growing or progressing. At some point you have to take a step forward. When you synchronise yourself with the powerful talents found in your Sun sign, you'll begin to understand what your mission in life will be. This is the true purpose and use of astrology.

So I invite you to gear up for an exciting fifteen months! Don't shrink back from life, even if at times some of the forecasts seem a little daunting. Don't forget that humans are always at their best when the going gets tough. The difficult planetary transits are merely invitations to bring out the best in yourself, while the favourable planetary cycles are seasons for enjoying the benefits that karma has in store for you.

Remain positive, expect the best, and see the beauty in everyone and everything. Remember the words of a great teacher: 'The world is as you see it.' In other words, life will reflect back to you only what you are willing to see.

I trust the coming fifteen months will grant you wonderful success, health, love and happiness. May the light of the Sun, the Moon and all of the stars fill your heart with joy and satisfaction.

Your Astrologer,

Dadhichi Toth

Contents

The Leo Identity 1

   Leo: A Snapshot 3

Star Sign Compatibility 25

2011: The Year Ahead 57

Your Bonus 2010
Three Month Forecast 71

   October 2010 73

   November 2010 78

   December 2010 83

2011: Month by Month Predictions 89

   January 2011 91

February 2011 96

March 2011 101

April 2011 106

May 2011 111

June 2011 116

July 2011 121

August 2011 126

September 2011 131

October 2011 136

November 2011 141

December 2011 146

2011: Astronumerology 151

2011: Your Daily Planner 175

The Leo Identity

LEO

THE LEO IDENTITY

A successful man is one who can lay a firm foundation with the bricks others have thrown at him

—David Brinkley

Leo: A Snapshot

Key Characteristics

Pioneering, commanding, inflexible, ambitious, loyal, physical, generous, regal

Compatible Star Signs

Aries, Sagittarius, Gemini, and Libra

Key Life Phrase

I Shine

Life Goals

To set an example to others and lead with integrity.

Platinum Assets

Great strength, vitality and magnetism

Zodiac Totem

The Lion

Zodiac Symbol

ᐃ

Zodiac Facts

Fifth sign of the zodiac, fixed, hot, masculine, dry

LEO

Element

Fire

Famous Leos

Monica Lewinsky, Jennifer Lopez, Kevin Spacey, Mick Jagger, Sandra Bullock, Arnold Schwarzenegger, Wesley Snipes, Coolio, Jerry Garcia, Yves Saint Laurent, Martha Stewart, Martin Sheen, David Duchovny, Dustin Hoffman, Melanie Griffith, Ben Affleck, Madonna, Robert De Niro, Robert Redford, Bill Clinton, Pete Sampras

Leo: Your profile

The power of the Sun is at the heart of your personality Leo, and as your ruling planet makes you shine so brightly in life. You therefore reflect these very traits of the star which is at the core of our solar system.

You are a mass of vibrant energy and display the qualities of the Sun in full measure. You are warm, intense and energetic. Therefore, you want to make an impression in everything you do—work, love and your social life as well.

Most Leos are extremely generous and give freely of their time, money and resources. But by the same token you expect others to reciprocate and to you loyalty is a two-way street. You also like to bring out the best in others. That's why when you see others holding back you find it hard to not to say something that will help them get out of their rut and become the best they can. You have a desire to see everyone give to the best of their ability. This

THE LEO IDENTITY

sometimes makes you appear a tyrant as your aspirations demand more than others can give.

You have an extraordinarily up-beat attitude and your positive mental disposition is one of your greatest assets. You don't let the negative influences of other people hold you back too much. You pride yourself on the fact that, even coming from humble beginnings, you're able to achieve everything you do through this single-minded positive attitude. You like to share this philosophy with others as well.

You often find yourself in the right place at the right time. Some people call this luck but you have the knack of knowing when to strike. You're able to maximise life's opportunities which is why others sometimes regard you with envy. But this doesn't worry you. You steam ahead irrespective of others' opinions.

Because you like to share your joys and successes you are sometimes unaware that people regard this as bragging. Some might even call you a show-off, but this is an incorrect opinion of you. Your dramatic flair is part and parcel of your in-built zest for life, love of people and optimistic attitude. Life to you is like a stage on which to perform and express your talents in full measure.

You exude charisma, creativity and a personal style all of your own. Like many who strut the stage of screen and music, you also want to be No.1 and present yourself as someone special with talents uniquely yours. Many high-profile celebrities and personalities are born under your sign of Leo, including Robert Redford, Bill Clinton, Pete Sampras and Madonna. All of them have made their mark in their own way and undoubtedly will remain the standard for others to follow.

Your honesty and integrity is your signature trademark and you are blunt in your openness at times. But people know you as a genuine friend who is always ready to give an honest answer. It seems that even if you can't help someone with their specific problem, you somehow still manage to exude a warm and reassuring vibration that makes them feel better for being with you.

You have a need to prove you are better than others which can sometimes be a problem for you. Humility should be cultivated if you are to sidestep problems in your relationships. You will be recognised for your dynamic energy and self-motivated action. You don't need to big-note yourself to others. People will instantly recognise your abilities and even look up to you. If this adulation begins to go to your head, you must listen to the cautionary advice of a good friend when s/he says, 'Get off your high horse, Leo!'

The lion is your totem and is lord of the jungle. Power, muscularity, grace and ferocity are some of the traits associated with this creature. Study it well to understand yourself better. You'll come to know that your physical appetites and general level of energy are extraordinarily high. It is no overstatement to say that you need to be physically mobile and fully engaged in meaningful work and social activities to feel good. You shine in almost anything you do and will, without any shadow of a doubt, make your mark in this world.

You are a born leader and people always look up to you for direction guidance and security. At times you are hard and demand excellence from them because you exhibit this in your own actions. People gravitate towards you and you will no doubt be capable of reaching the zenith of whatever activity you choose in your life.

You tend to be a leader in your field because you have such a pioneering spirit which is also tied in with your desire to be the best. On the one hand you're quite happy to pursue a life in which you follow the rules and regulations of others but you by far prefer to blaze your own trail through the jungles of life.

It is through this attitude you will carve your own niche and make that name for yourself. Either way, you cannot help but be noticed and make an impression everywhere you go. This is the majesty and royal bearing of your star sign—Leo.

Three classes of Leo

Being born between the 24th of July and the 5th of August makes you Leo through and through. Your charisma and power are undeniable and from an early age you have had a strong sense of your

LEO

personal destiny. As a result don't be surprised to find yourself assuming positions of authority and power in life. Some of you may even hold high office, become interested in politics or community work and will certainly become the best in your field.

As a Leo born between the 6th and the 14th of August you have an adventurous nature and like to explore the different avenues of life to make your journey more exciting and interesting. Culture, travel and higher studies are some of the different avenues which will draw you away from a conventional lifestyle to an independent type of existence. You have a great love of freedom and will never let anyone dictate the terms of your being.

Impatience and a hot-headed nature are some of the problems you face being born between the 15th and the 23rd of August. Once you can bring these emotions under control you have a much better chance of not only being successful but finding happiness in your personal affairs as well. Because of the strong influence of Mars and Aries on your birthday you have a strong ego and need to understand that others may just be right sometimes. Notwithstanding these negative traits, you do have a very generous nature and are affectionate to the ones you care for.

Leo role model: Robert De Niro

Robert De Niro is born under the sign of Leo and is a powerful presence on screen and off. His Leo traits reflect perfectly the commanding nature of those born under this regal star sign.

The life of an actor is never easy even for those who have great talent but once again the tenacity and vision of Leo are seen in the life and times of Robert De Niro. Just like this Leo relative of yours, you are destined for big things as long as you allow your vision to take shape and remain committed to your destiny.

Leo: The light side

You seem to bring a ray of sunshine with you wherever you go. This is the reason you are loved by others and your presence is always welcome. If others feel down, you have the uncanny knack of being able to lift their spirits even without saying too much.

People often wonder where you get so much physical energy and vitality from. This is due to the rulership of the Sun on your birth date which gives you an immense power, recuperative abilities and the tenacity to achieve your goals. You never take no for an answer. Learn to give a little bit to yourself, however, and don't overdo things. You have a tendency to push yourself to the limits.

You know how to lead and others take pleasure in you taking on that role. In you they feel secure and know that you will look after their best interests. Once you set your mind on something you never let go. This is also why many Leo born individuals become so successful in life.

LEO

Leo: The shadow side

You have this tendency to assume that your opinions are superior to others. This can make you unpopular even though you mean well. Yes often you are correct but you must understand that the way you present information is often more of an influence than the content of what you're saying.

Leo is a fixed sign which means that you are often inflexible in changing your attitudes and values and this must also be carefully monitored especially in long-term relationships otherwise it will put pressure on others to always adjust themselves to you rather than ensuring that mutual change is the basis of your partnership.

Try not to overwork as well. Many Leos in their attempt to give their loved ones the best, end up spending far too much time away from their families. You're loyal, protective and loving of your children and family but must also learn that money and status are not the only things that they need. Give them time as well.

Leo woman

You will agree that everyone is unique but there is some reason Leo women seem just that little bit more unique. An unusual blend of pride, elegance and charm make you very much your own person. It's hard not to notice you when you walk in the room. There is something regal and majestic about your manner. I've found that even the women born

THE LEO IDENTITY

under Leo from somewhat modest circumstances possess that special 'something'.

You possess all the hallmarks of class and grace, and always believe that you are marked for some sort of special destiny, for bigger and better things. You know how to hold yourself and this single quality is extremely alluring to members of the opposite sex. Leo women turn heads and will have their fair share of potential mates in life.

As the lioness of the zodiac, power is one of your favourite games and you win when you play it. You have a clear idea of what you want and you know how to go about getting it. You have no problem mixing with and even dominating members of either sex. You are straightforward with both men and women and are fearless in the face of challenge or adversity.

You dislike any form of weakness and see it as a demeaning characteristic. You instinctively understand Darwin's law of survival of the fittest. Perhaps this is why you understand that if you exhibit weakness it's likely you will lose your prize position as leader to someone less capable than yourself.

You look to others for power as well. You must be in friendships and relationships of equality otherwise you feel ineffectual. It is not enough for you to dominate others because you prefer a sharing of power and if the person is a little weaker than you, but prepared to lift their ball game, you enjoy the challenge of helping them become better people. This will be one of the main motivating factors for your choice of friends, business colleagues and most importantly the romantic or marriage partners you choose to spend your life with. You can't handle impotence in any shape or form. You expect people to exhibit the same, if not greater, strength, than yourself.

I have no doubt that just as the lioness in the jungle often leads the solitary life, some Leo women prefer to remain alone rather than settle for second best. In this way you are a rather uncompromising woman. The fact is that if a person can't be bothered to deal with you on your terms, you're quite happy to remain by yourself.

Because you're born under the fire element, creativity is very high on your agenda and you therefore love to express your feelings and your character through fashionable statements. You see this as a perfect expression of yourself, not to mention the fact that it is also a lot of fun. Bright and dramatic colours are your style, and fashion combinations serve to enhance your already attractive personality. You can't handle being overlooked! But please don't overcompensate, especially if you're middle-aged, because mutton dressed as lamb doesn't go over that well.

Sometimes, you will have to deal with people who don't like your brutal honesty and your life will be sprinkled with episodes of contention and opposition. You don't mind this and thrive on the excitement of doing battle and winning. You are a friend for life, but expect the same loyalty

THE LEO IDENTITY

in return. And, of course, the flip side is that you make a most formidable enemy. It's therefore best for people to remain on your friendlier side.

Leadership comes easily to you and you naturally gravitate towards positions in which you can assume authority in some capacity. Success is a clear focus for Leo women. They often achieve it too.

Leo man

Leo is one of the most masculine signs of the zodiac and men born during this period of the year exhibit male personality traits in full.

As a Leo male you are hot-natured, bombastic, forceful, ready for action and sometimes inflexible. But you are also enormously affectionate and dedicated. You're caring, demonstrative and lovable. As Leo also rules the zone of children, you are youthful in your exuberance for life and your character reflects a child-like innocence at times.

Your character is contradictory sometimes. You are hard to understand because you are so proud yet at the same time so generous. Pride and power to you are personal statements about what matters in life. Success underpins your motivation in everything you do. You need to be the best.

Because you are audacious and daring others try to model their lives on your example. Your self-confidence and positive thinking is certainly an inspiration to others. You really want to inject this

LEO

enthusiasm into everyone you come in contact with, but because others don't often have the same high level of self-esteem that you do, they misinterpret your motives as ego driven unfortunately.

You always live your life to very high principles and many you live and work with find it hard to meet your expectations. You see in them what they can't and you often encourage them to do their best. This is why you make a great leader and mentor. Your desire to drag everyone up to this unattainable benchmark makes you irritable and frustrated. If you're a dad, you are far too demanding and expect the impossible from kids who just don't have the same commitment to principle or ambition as you do.

Try to be more compassionate and less demanding. Understand that others can't all be as strong as you. No doubt your intentions are noble, but if this isn't working for you, what's the point? Openly or behind your back, others admire you for your dynamic energy and wish they were like you. When you sense this in another person, you have no hesitation in giving them your assistance. Be careful that people don't take advantage of your good nature, however.

You are confident due to your successes. Hang on...even if you aren't yet successful you know you will be so your self-assurance never seems to wane! There is a passive strength and self-control that emanates success. Be careful vanity doesn't overtake you by surprise. Be more humble.

THE LEO IDENTITY

You are intensely protective of the ones you love. You'll never leave your family unless there are extreme reasons for doing so. You measure your success somewhat by what you can provide others. Your security is a source of strength to friends and family alike. Marriage is the perfect way for you to express your loyal Leo qualities.

Leo child

For the most part, children of Leo are quite a happy bunch being infused by the vital rays of the sun, their ruling planet. They love to play, compete and express themselves in a positive manner.

Leo children do have an insatiable need to be recognised, to be the centre of attention and may sometimes dominate their peer group. Handling in this aspect of their personalities may require quiet cleverness on the part of their parents. Remember, however, never undermine them, particularly in front of their friends, as this can create long-term problems for them.

Leo children have natural leadership ability and like to assert themselves over their friends. You need to teach them the value of sharing power and also serving. As an old mentor of mine once used to remark 'let he who has served first command'. If not checked early, they may become tyrannical in their friendships, expecting everyone to bow down to their every whim.

Because of their competitive nature, Leo children enjoy sports which will allow them to prove their capabilities. Any type of fast sport which requires tenacity and strength will bring out their superior talents. Often, the Leo's sporting agenda becomes part of the family routine and can create a great deal of joy and bonding for all the family members. Physical activity will enhance their vital life force.

You must always provide your little Leo loads of loving attention and affection. They love being the centre of attention and being the object of your adoration, so any gestures of love naturally make them feel great.

If you offer love and heartfelt tenderness to your Leo child, you will see that beneath the roaring exterior is a lifelong loyal and devoted friend.

Romance, love and marriage

Astrologically speaking the main domain of Leo is that of love affairs, entertainment and other pleasurable pursuits. This is the fifth zone of the zodiac and the natural sign of romance and creativity. Love and the joy of social life is one of the most important attributes of your nature and this is inherent in your personality.

The fact that you are usually a happy-go-lucky type of person means that love is never far away from you. You connect with others socially and romantically in a very easy way and always find yourself in the company of the opposite sex without too much effort on your part. The thrill of conquest is an instinctive urge of the lion in both male and female of this zodiac sign. Finding your perfect

THE LEO IDENTITY

soulmate may not be an easy task however. You are not easy to please and believe that you deserve better than you usually get.

You must never rush making a commitment and in fact it doesn't particularly concern you. You're quite happy to enjoy life and explore the diverse people that come your way. Sexual exploits are an important part of your life too. This is more pronounced if you happen to be a Leo male. Sexuality is to you a form of creative expression.

You dominate social situations. If you do this with your usual group of friends they usually overlook this personality trait. When you're in a group of strangers and try to control the situation however they may not take too kindly to this and see you as trying to muscle in on their territory particularly if love is at stake.

Often I have found Leo doesn't find their soulmate till after they have experienced many friendships and affairs of the heart. Satisfaction in love may not be achieved until midlife. This is because Saturn and Uranus are ruling your marriage sector. Saturn is an older planet and Uranus is progressive. Delays may be the result of this combination.

When you finally do connect with your soulmate, you do so with considerable commitment. You have staying power due to the fact that Leo is a fixed sign of the zodiac. And you love ferociously with loyalty, affection and protection. You are territorial about the ones you love as well. Don't allow possessiveness to get the better of you in marriage

LEO

or long-term relationships though. This will unravel the trust and commitment you have with that special person.

You set very high standards for others if they choose to enter into a relationship with you and this can be a tall order for lesser mortals whose love may not be quite as intense and demanding as yours. Be patient and a little more forgiving of others. You can be a wonderful teacher Leo so 'show not tell'.

You have an impeccable dress sense and are always aware of the impression you make. You dress to attract others especially if you have your eye on someone in particular. You arouse envy since you stand out from others and can sometimes be seen as treading on their turf. To avoid this, you could try underplaying your showmanship. You'll still achieve the object of your desire.

You are very black and white in your relationships and will see your partner as either an asset or liability. It's not that you see a lover as an accessory but to you it is vitally important to have the support you need in a social and professional context. You want your partner to be part of that—to enhance your status and the perception of yourself in the eyes of others. You'll soon look elsewhere for someone to reciprocate the effort, loyalty and love you offer if you don't find it in someone.

When you finally marry and connect with your soul-mate at the heart and spirit level, you're determined to make good your commitment to the sacred vows of matrimony. To you, marriage is

THE LEO IDENTITY

a lifelong commitment and you're going to give it your best shot. On these terms, love will make Leo extremely happy and fulfilled.

Health, wellbeing and diet

Health should never be too much of an issue for you Leo, as long as you don't overdo it either in terms of your day-to-day activities or your diet. Leo is a strong, healthy and robust sign. You must appreciate your health and not take it for granted however.

Because of your strong sense of wellbeing, sport and outdoor activities enhance your health. As a fire sign, physical mobility is essential to maintaining and increasing your wellness. Remember, however, that your constitution is very hot due to the Sun's rulership and you often overheat yourself through mental, physical and dietary excess. Moderation will overcome this.

You always take up a challenge but sometimes for the wrong reasons. You mustn't let your ego dominate your activities. You must be especially careful not to be over reactive to people who are competitive in nature. This triggers your ego to prove that you can do better. Set some limits for yourself in all these areas so that it doesn't undermine your wellbeing.

Leo rules the spine, back and heart so these parts of your body will be naturally weak and susceptible to problems. There may be a tendency to backache, spinal curvature through poor posture, and cardiovascular issues later in life. Try to avoid extremes in exercise and sport that may over-tax your body generally.

You love hot, spicy tastes and food and these may also cause problems to your digestion. While your metabolism burns up most of what you eat quickly, there's a tendency to eat red meats (like your totem, the lion). You must therefore eat leaner and less fattening foods. Alkaline foods will help neutralise the excess acidity in your system.

If you must eat meat try adding a variety of wholegrain foods, fresh vegetables and other less processed foods. Because you're also excessive in many of your habits and this includes eating, learn to eat less. Leo, the lion, does have a tendency to gorge and then sleep all day. Grazing throughout the day is preferable to overeating at any given meal.

Lime juice, chamomile and fenugreek herbs are excellent tonics for you. Papaya, mango, banana and other yellow or gold-coloured fruits are nourishing for your system. Orange vegetables, including pumpkin, are first-rate pick-me-ups. Wholegrain rice and other steamed foods supplement your vitality and health. Fenugreek is also an excellent herb to reduce or remove toxins from your body.

Work

The worst thing that can happen to you in your professional life is to be overlooked, unrecognised

THE LEO IDENTITY

or unappreciated for the work that you do. Mostly, you do good work but as a Leo-born individual you certainly need to feel successful and to be applauded for your input.

You achieve your ambitions because you are so determined and are not easily discouraged from the goals you set yourself. By the same token you're well aware of the benefits that the power and glory bring when achieving your goals.

The planet ruling your profession is Venus, and she makes you passionate, extravagant and also creative. Saturn who also has a say in your professional destiny indicates that you need concentration as well in order to balance extra-vagances in your work routine. Some Leo-born natives become workaholics

In whatever line of work you choose to exert yourself, you'll more than likely rise to an executive position, or at least senior management level. You could become a CEO of a company, a sportsperson, government department executive, secretarial worker or teacher.

You have great dramatic flair which is why theatrical opportunities are possible. You would make a wonderful actor, musician or even screenplay writer or film technician. If you are less interested in traditional office-style work, the outdoors and nature are wonderful environments for your work. Forest ranger, horticulturist and sports instructor will be fine creative outlets for you.

LEO

Key to karma, spirituality and emotional balance

Your Leo patterning suggests that you are aggressive in the way you attempt to achieve your goals in life. Strength and leadership, which things you aspire to, may ultimately be your biggest challenges in life and have their roots in some deep, karmic past issues.

Your key words are 'I Shine' and because you have a very powerful soul force, your spiritual aptitude is strong. As you reach midlife you will start to fill your practical affairs with a spiritual and generous quality. Sharing your successes will give you great pleasure.

On Sundays and Thursdays connect with your inner powers of intuition and psychic abilities. Ruby and Garnet are helpful gemstones for Leo.

Your lucky days

Your luckiest days are Sundays, Mondays, Tuesdays and Thursdays.

Your lucky numbers

Remember that the forecasts given later in the book will help you optimise your chances of winning. Your lucky numbers are:

1, 10, 19, 28, 37, 46, 55

3, 12, 21, 30, 39, 48, 57

9, 18, 27, 36, 45, 54, 63

Your destiny years

Your most important years are: 1, 10, 19, 28, 37, 46, 55, 64, 73 and 82.

LEO

Star Sign Compatibility

STAR SIGN COMPATIBILITY

Experience is the child of thought, and thought is the child of action

—Benjamin Disraeli

Romantic compatibility

How compatible are you with your current partner, lover or friend? Did you know that astrology can reveal a whole new level of understanding between people and their relationships. Simply by looking at their star sign and that of their partner. In this chapter I'd like to show you how to better appreciate your strengths and challenges using Sun sign compatibility.

The Sun reflects your drive, willpower and personality. The essential qualities of two star signs blend like two pure colours producing an entirely new colour. Relationships, similarly, produce their own emotional colours when two people interact. The following is a general guide to your romantic prospects with others and how, by knowing the astrological 'colour' of each other, the art of love can help you create a masterpiece.

When reading the following I ask you to remember that no two star signs are ever *totally* incompatible. With effort and compromise, even the most 'difficult' astrological matches can work. Don't close your mind to the full range of life's possibilities! Learning about each other and ourselves is the most important facet of astrology.

Each star sign combination is followed by the

LEO

elements of those star signs and the result of their combining. For instance, Aries is a fire sign and Aquarius is an air sign and this combination produces a lot of 'hot air'. Air feeds fire and fire warms air. In fact, fire requires air. However, not all air and fire combinations work. I have included information about the different birth periods within each star sign and this will throw even more light on your prospects for a fulfilling love life with any star sign you choose.

Good luck in your search for love, and may the stars shine upon you in 2011!

Compatibility quick-reference guide

Each of the twelve star signs has a greater or lesser affinity with one another. The quick reference guide will show you who's hot and who's not so hot as far as your relationships are concerned.

LEO + ARIES
Fire + Fire = Explosion

There are some star signs which get on OK. There are some that get on terribly! Yet again there are matches which are truly supreme. In the case of Leo and Aries the astrological verdict is that you are remarkably well suited as a coupe and friends. The factor which you both share is the element of fire. You are both enormously creative and this points to a very collaborative union for you. The two of you will have many mutually rewarding times.

STAR SIGN COMPATIBILITY

Quick-reference guide: Horoscope compatibility between signs (percentage)

	Aries	Taurus	Gemini	Cancer	Leo	Virgo	Libra	Scorpio	Sagittarius	Capricorn	Aquarius	Pisces
Aries	60	65	70	65	90	45	70	80	90	50	55	65
Taurus	60	70	70	80	70	90	75	85	50	95	80	85
Gemini	70	70	75	60	80	75	90	60	75	50	90	50
Cancer	65	80	60	75	70	80	60	95	55	45	90	90
Leo	90	70	80	70	85	70	65	75	95	45	70	75
Virgo	45	90	75	75	75	70	80	85	70	95	50	70
Libra	70	75	90	60	65	80	80	85	80	85	95	50
Scorpio	80	85	60	95	75	85	85	90	85	65	60	95
Sagittarius	90	50	75	55	95	70	80	80	85	55	60	75
Capricorn	50	95	50	45	45	95	85	65	55	85	70	85
Aquarius	55	80	90	70	70	50	95	60	60	70	80	55
Pisces	65	85	50	90	75	70	50	95	75	85	55	80

LEO

You are both high-powered individuals with imaginative impulses and will support each other. Together you will propel each other in achieving your life ambitions. Aries must understand that you are a proud and dominating individual not unlike them. Who will rule the roost? That is a question you will both have to confront in this very potent relationship.

The two of you together can be an explosive match. One of you will eventually burn out the other, mostly with your strongly competitive urges. Because Leo is the fifth sign, it indicates a playful and sporting association between you both though. Try to keep it all in good fun. As both of you make strong leaders you will have to determine who is going to lead. The two of you must learn how to share that responsibility. Neither of you are submissive, so this will challenge you.

A relationship between you ensures a rich and rewarding experience, sexually and emotionally. This is a compatible astrological combination from a sexual point of view, that's for sure. There's a creative spark in your intimate connection as fire is spontaneous, fresh and ever youthful.

If there's any problem in this respect, it would most likely be your over-indulgence in sexual activity together. Are you complaining Leo? No way and neither will Aries!

You'll find yourself fascinated by those Aries born between the 21st and the 30th of March as they are ruled by Mars and this implies strong karmic associations between you. You have the opportunity to dedicate loads of time to long-distance travel and exciting cultural interchanges with them. It appears that this association will be one predominately focused on exploration and fun.

Most Arians are compatible with Leo, but the best are those born between the 31st of March and the 10th of April where the solar qualities are enhanced. You will automatically be drawn to these people and can develop a strong friendship, which like good wine, matures with age.

Those Aries born between the 11th and the 20th of April are partly ruled by Jupiter as well as Mars and this suggests some very exciting and attractive romance between you. Of all the Aries you meet, this group will more than likely appeal to you sexually.

Entertainment, sports and other playful activities seem to be natural to both of you and will liven up your relationship together. Aries born during this period also have an innate wisdom that attracts you. They are able to settle your fiery and inflexible disposition due to the co-rulership of Jupiter.

LEO + TAURUS
Fire + Earth = Lava

This is a combination that works in some cases yet in others doesn't. You need to be very clever in understanding each other and making allowances

LEO

for each other's differences. No doubt, the powers of attraction between you are strong and so therefore the two of you will want to explore your connection more deeply.

Socially you are both quite active and your attractive personalities will be forever trying to outdo each other for the attention of others. This will be entertaining for a period of time but eventually a clash of wills and a battle of egos could result.

The Sun and Venus, your ruling planets respectively, according to some astrologers are not particularly comfortable with each other. There is however a strong attraction between you and this is very palpable. Others notice it as well. Leo, you are the bright shining star and Taurus, the sensual, earthy sign of love.

You are extremely protective of your Taurean partner and this is associated with your totem the lion. The lion is thoroughly committed to providing and nurturing his or her clan. Taurus will be irresistibly drawn to this fact and will feel as though you can provide them with the security and confidence that they instinctively need.

Leo, you do tend to stimulate the emotional and sexual desires of your Taurean partner. Even if you can't sustain this in the long term, at least for a period of time you will experience great pleasure together. You're advised to move a little more slowly if you've just met each other as your passionate drive could sweep both of you off your feet. Take things a step at a time and if you can both balance those pleasure-seeking attributes with practical, nurturing traits, this could well be a relationship offering you permanence.

Seductive and loving Taureans born between the 20th and the 29th of April find you hard to resist. But these are the slow moving Taureans who are extremely fixed in their opinions and manner of doing things. You could become frustrated with their inflexible attitudes and their desire to change the way you think.

Your most fitting match especially where love is concerned, is with those Taureans born between the 30th of April and the 10th of May, as they activate your social interests. Interestingly, because they also have a strong connection with your financial or business affairs—as Mercury connects them to your finances—you can enjoy love, social life and financial benefits in your association with these people.

You have a reasonably good chance of making a go of it with Taureans born between the 11th and the 21st of May. One thing you both share in common is this incredible element of protection and loyalty. In terms of making a life together, and growing a family, this is something that you will each appreciate in the other and should work very well at together.

LEO + GEMINI
Fire + Air = Hot Air

After the same element of your Sun sign, which is fire, the next best elemental combination for you is with those born under the element of air. With air and fire we find an exciting and progressive style of relationship. Leo and Gemini fall under this elemental category. Because Gemini is essentially an intellectual and articulate sign, their mental versatility will fan the flames of your fiery Leo pride.

You will find in Gemini a most interesting friend and companion and will want to spend a great deal of time with them. Your relationship will work very well with Gemini because their star sign also happens to be in your sector of friendship. This is undeniably a great social, intellectual and emotional match.

You have a very warm and enthusiastic personality and Gemini finds it hard not to be attracted to and love this quality of your character. You give them a sense that their skills and talents are appreciated. You're able to encourage them even in the detailed aspects of life. In a social context you are both great company. You do tend to be a hard taskmaster occasionally though, expecting a very high standard from your Gemini partner. Give them some scope to develop themselves independently.

Gemini has a great ability to understand a diverse range of facts and figures and will often

STAR SIGN COMPATIBILITY

surprise you with the sheer volume of information that they can cram into their brains. Unfortunately, many born under Gemini seem to be Jacks-of-all-trades and masters of none, in your opinion. Part of your challenge will be to anchor the flighty Gemini character and help them deepen their knowledge of one, rather than many topics.

Geminis born between the 22nd of May and the 1st of June will have a knack of business and finance. You may meet someone in this category through your working associations. A relationship with them will centre on money and probability. Acquiring money together will be a very pleasurable activity you can share. This commendation should provide you a good and comfortable lifestyle.

Geminis born between the 2nd and the 12th of June are particularly attractive to you and will complement you in a social context. However, the long-term influence of work dominating their lifestyle may be uncompromising for the two of you.

Saturn, the co-ruling planet of this group of Geminis is not particularly lucky for your health and physical wellbeing. These Gemini-born individuals can affect your life force adversely and will tire you out. You should only take these Geminis in small doses.

Any Gemini born between the 13th and the 21st of June could provide you a great basis for a long-term romance. Aquarius and Uranus co-rule them and make them exciting but also a little unpredictable. This group of Geminis is suited to marriage with you. You will be suddenly attracted to these individuals and may meet them in the most amazing and unexpected circumstances.

LEO + CANCER
Fire + Water = Steam

It's not a good idea to use a relationship with Cancer as a means of sorting out your emotional shortcomings. At first it might be easy to be lured by the loving affection of Cancer. Often, however, this attraction is a little mismatched and Cancer, you will soon learn, lacks the self-confidence and inner assurance that you so abundantly strut. This initially seems like a great coming together of opposites, but may become a drain on your mental resources.

Leo and Cancer represent the archetypal male and female principles in nature. As a result it is quite usual for you to be attracted to each other. Although these principles appear to be opposed, the blending of two such forces in nature gives rise to the process of creation at every level. There can, therefore, be a strong karmic link between you.

Fire heats water and ultimately creates steam if the heat's on for too long. Water has the power to quell and dampen your hot nature Leo. This is the basic interplay of elements that is at the heart of your Leo/Cancer combination. What this really means however is that each of you must allow the other space and time to simply be yourselves and not judge each other too harshly.

Don't try to dominate Cancer. You need to use reverse psychology with them. If you give them space, they'll be drawn to you. The more you try to control them the more they will recoil. They may appear to be weak-natured but possess resilience, strength and independence.

Cancerians born between the 22nd of June and the 3rd of July may be a group of individuals you don't easily connect with; you will feel they are a little too weird and 'left of the dial' for your tastes. You won't feel much attraction to them. For some reason you will also feel as though they don't have the oomph and get up and go physically that you would like to see in a partner in life. Cancerians born between the 4th and the 13th of July may come across as somewhat stubborn and a little too emotional for you to handle. But you'll still feel a magnetic attraction to them. Tread cautiously, because these waters will be out of your depth.

This overemotional aspect to Cancer will leave you feeling emotionally drained. You'll need to learn how to resonate on the same level with them and this will take considerable flexibility by both of you.

Cancerians born between the 14th and the 23rd of July brings karmic opportunities to the table if you choose to become involved with them. They have a wonderfully generous nature and this resonates well with you. A great interplay of energies can be expected if you choose to spend time with them.

LEO + LEO
Fire + Fire = Explosion

Leo with another Leo is like stars coming together and creating a supernova. This combination is bright, attractive, charming and full of lifelong opportunities both socially and materially. You are both ruled by the Sun and this has great benefits in terms of vitality, intellectual interplay and social satisfaction. One thing however, you will be constantly vying for attention by trying to outdo each other. You don't need an astrologer to tell you that Leo is one of the most self absorbed signs and pride is part of the Leo nature.

This is a majestic, bright and vibrant relationship that will give you great happiness, excitement and at times tension as well. But at least it will never be boring. Both of you are driven by strong egos and this, to my way of seeing it, is the biggest issue for the relationship notwithstanding the great compatibility ratio that is inherent in this astrological match. Two proud and obstinate individuals must learn the lesson of yielding at some point or other. Give and take is the key to making this a supremely satisfying relationship.

Often people have a problem when I tell them that the relationship can prove to be demanding on them. But this is not such a bad thing for either of you Leo lovers, because these demands you place on each other will be the very stuff that pushes you to become better people, to grow and to achieve the things in life that you feel have meaning. Together you will goad each other on to bigger and better things. And in this way, you appreciate the challenges of the relationship with your Leo siblings.

You are suited to each other sexually, knowing just how to offer the right dramatic touch to take lovemaking to another level. You are both natural lovers and like the idea of entertaining and pleasuring the other. Sexuality is never boring for Leo. Because Leo rules the fifth sign of the natural zodiac, entertainment, sport and other such activities are your forte.

In your relationship with any Leo born between the 24th of July and the 4th of August you will both be particularly stubborn and possibly too stuck in your ways of doing things, particularly if you have reached midlife and don't necessarily want to change the way you do things. This would have to be one of the most inflexible combinations in the zodiac.

Leos born between the 5th and the 14th of August are a less dominant breed: expansive, honest and welcoming. You'll have great love and friendship with them. There is also a strong sense of loyalty amongst these individuals. These people value loyalty like you.

Leos born between the 15th and the 23rd of August, challenge you completely because Mars has a strong sway over their destiny. Expect intense and feisty clashes, interspersed with timely, spiritual interludes. This group of Leos is the most complex, but their spontaneity will most likely stimulate you but at the same time be a cause for concern.

LEO + VIRGO
Fire + Earth = Lava

You could easily overlook Virgo if you were looking for a partner that stimulates you, excites you and somewhat reflects your own dramatic flair for life. And this is because Virgo is a rather timid and humble personality. But as I always say, you must never judge a book by its cover. In the first instance Virgo could easily be overwhelmed by your forceful personality, Leo. But they have their own subtle type of power so you must learn not to abuse the power and control you possess.

You'll find Virgo full of strength in their own way although less forceful or obvious than Leo. Just because they have a tendency to work behind the scenes in a really exacting and self-sacrificial manner doesn't mean that they are a pushover. Unlike you they are not so interested in how they come across as in how well they execute their professional work and daily duties.

In your dealings with Virgo you must understand that they have a particular penchant for detail. You'll have to get on the same page as them with this or this could cause problems. You're a big picture person who likes to see the totality and could feel rather annoyed when Virgo tries to point out how, when and where you should do what you do.

Before you start to give up on considering a relationship with Virgo let me say that there are some redeeming features in this relationship. Virgo is uplifted by your warm and passionate personality. But the same can't be said for your experience of Virgo. They are constantly preoccupied with details and hygiene and seem to be just so in everything they do. In terms of lovemaking, this will irritate you. You prefer a roaring good time between the sheets to the more modest display of Virgo.

You'll find Virgos born between the 24th of August and the 2nd of September less high-strung than most of their Virgo brothers and sisters. You can therefore become good friends with these individuals. You can share some fine times with them and in the appropriate manner bring them out of their shells and start to see a side to their nature that is actually quite endearing to you.

Virgos born between the 3rd and the 12th of September are rather sober type individuals as a result of the influence Saturn and Capricorn have on their birth dates. You require fun, warmth and openness to be fulfilled in your love life and unfortunately these people tend to be quite the opposite. They are quite cautious and less spontaneous than you'd prefer in a partner.

Without a doubt any Virgo born between the 13th and the 22nd of September will magnetically draw you to them and leave you wanting more. Once you get to know them however you could find that their dominant personalities do tend to clash with your own. Unless you're prepared to compromise and submit to some of their bossy ways, this relationship will not be all that inspiring.

LEO + LIBRA
Fire + Air = Hot Air

Because Libra is ruled by the planet of love, Venus, this is the key word and colours everything they say and do. They are social personalities and love to be with others. Their warmth and vitality is not unlike yours. They have a very varied view of life and can fit in with almost anyone they meet. Because of this similarity in your personalities the two of you will naturally be drawn to each other and can expect to forge a great friendship.

Librans are diplomatic individuals and this is also another trait which makes them loved. The scales of justice which just happens to be their totem doesn't adequately reflect the imbalance they feel within themselves. Their striving for balance is what brings them in touch with so many people. In their search for equilibrium, harmony and love, they seek out the best in others as well as advice that can help steer them in the right direction. You must never take advantage of this with your Libran partner as they are also extremely sensitive and often never recover from any sort of deception. They are vulnerable by nature.

Your honesty is noteworthy but probably needs a hand from Libra's more polished way of presenting the cold hard truth. As well, your words may be too harsh for the delicate and sensitive ears of Libra. The Sun and Venus make you an extremely eye-catching couple. You possess charisma and your energies act like a magnet to draw people to you. This is a lucky combination.

As the two of you get to know each other, you realise your common interests include such things as hosting parties, dinners and other functions within the home that will make your domestic life a real social vortex of fun activities. Spending time and furthering your interests with friends and colleagues will be something you'll support each other in. Generally your sexual encounters with Librans will be quite enjoyable for the above reasons.

Any relationship with Librans born between the 23rd of September and the 3rd of October would suit you quite well. These Librans are always on the go and could actually make you dizzy after a time. Unless you're prepared to jet set and do a lot of travel you're probably best to keep these Librans at arm's length.

There is a very strong karmic attraction for you with Librans born between the 4th and the 13th of October. These lovely and sometimes slightly zany

Librans have a strong influence from Uranus which means they provide you perfect marriage material. You'll feel extremely attracted to them and will enjoy their progressive thinking and spontaneous independence.

Most Librans born between the 14th and the 23rd of October are reasonably compatible with you. You'll develop a wonderful relationship with these people as they're co-ruled by Mercury and Gemini. They are also a little enigmatic as Mercury is a convertible planet and shows that their moods change constantly. They'll definitely keep you on your toes.

LEO + SCORPIO
Fire + Water = Steam

You tend to generally draw people to you who possess considerable power and energy to achieve the things in life that they aspire to. This is why you're immediately attracted to those born under the star sign of Scorpio. Just like a Scorpio you possess an incredibly powerful will. There is a lot of mutual respect between Leo and Scorpio for this reason.

You're both inflexible and Scorpio's icy nature needs a little time to thaw under your sunny rays of sunshine. If, however, you're patient enough they will come around and show you the softer and more sensitive side of their nature. Scorpio is sensual, emotional and very intense. Scorpio attracts you and draws you into a powerful emotional relationship with them.

Scorpio also has a depth and spiritual fascination with such things as death and the afterlife. If some of these topics unnerve you and seem far too deep psychologically, you may have to ask Scorpio to back-off for a while. You have a tremendous respect for Scorpio's deeply probing mind and you'll also want to prove your worth in this psychological realm.

You must understand the Scorpio is not only interested in having a relationship with you physically and emotionally. They need to connect with you on the deepest spiritual level as well. This complexity of association might not be easy for you to deal with. But unless you get your head around this, your relationship may fizzle out and you will unfortunately miss out on the incredible experience that a Scorpio love affair has to offer.

Although Leo and Scorpio are not the best astrological matches, I have known star signs from both sides to feel quite gratified in their sexual expression together. Of course, when we talk of compatibility astrologically, we can simply generalise on each and every aspect of the relationship. Strangely, your sexual tastes seem to be quite compatible.

Scorpios born between the 24th of October and the 2nd of November are particularly powerful and intense. They have strong sexual appetites and will exert their passionate influences over you

LEO

but I don't think you'll be complaining about this will you, Leo?

Scorpios born between the 3rd and the 12th of November are quite well suited to a relationship with you. In particular if you are born between the 5th and the 14th of August this compatibility is increased. For other Leos there can be some conflict and even confusion so they are best avoided for the purpose of any long-term, committed relationship.

Scorpio is not quite as up-front in displaying their control and power. You outwardly wish to exert your dominance but this could be the wrong tactic in a relationship with them. That is particularly so with those born between the 13th and the 22nd of November. They are a gentler breed of Scorpio and your overbearing ways may be a little too hard for them to handle.

LEO + SAGITTARIUS
Fire + Fire = Explosion

Once again we come across the fire-fire combination which is an excellent match astrologically speaking. Yes, Sagittarius like you is born under the same elements and is a no-brainer! The Leo-Sagittarius combination is very hard to beat as far as relationships are concerned. The warmth and power they radiate is appreciated by you and reflects your own frank honesty. Very few star signs can handle the blunt approach of Sagittarius, but a fire sign such as yours is an exception.

STAR SIGN COMPATIBILITY

You have an intuitive connection with Sagittarians and therefore you feel as if you know them intimately even after your first meeting or two. It's instant recognition with this one, that's for sure. You mirror each others' enthusiasm for life and enjoy what each other has to offer.

Sagittarians are always on the go. They will introduce you to their world and should inspire you to travel, explore and discover life generally. This will fill you with light and warmth and also fulfil them to the heart of their being. Generally the Sagittarian's ruthlessly honest tongue would inflict deep wounds on your proud Leo ego. But this is not likely, because you don't feel their honesty is meant to hurt, but rather to uplift and improve.

Sagittarians are enthusiastic, generous and easy-going for the most part. You feel comfortable with them and your day-to-day activities gel quite well. They may however seem to be a little less committed than you when it comes to the long term. They need just a little more time than you. In the first stages of your love life with them, just try to get into the slipstream of the Sagittarian lifestyle and relax a little.

Leo is proud but Sagittarius sometimes has little concern for the feelings of others in dishing out the truth. You have to learn to take as good as you give because just like Leo, Sagittarius is concerned with the truth and telling it as it is.

There's a creative spark in your sexual coming together, as fire is spontaneous, fresh and creative.

LEO

Your sexual intimacy should be invigorating and loving. This is truly one of the better combinations in the zodiac.

Exciting love affairs are destined to occur with those born between the 23rd of November and the 1st of December. Both the level of passion and the intensity and frequency of your desires will seem to be perfectly suited to these people. There will certainly be no problem in your physical compatibility if you choose these loving Sagittarians.

There is a deep knowing as well as a deep longing to be with Sagittarians born between the 2nd and the 11th of December. There are strong karmic forces at work with these individuals and yourself. Special spiritual insights and lessons will spring from Sagittarians born in this period. They may be instrumental in dramatically transforming your life.

Sagittarians who are born between the 12th and the 21st of December spark your deepest emotional responses, due to the common co-rulership of their sign by the Sun and Leo. With these people you can truly be yourself, in fact your *best* self.

LEO + CAPRICORN
Fire + Earth = Lava

I always feel a little guilty when I don't give two star signs the thumbs up. But my job here in writing to you is to lay the cards out on the table for you

STAR SIGN COMPATIBILITY

based upon sound astrological principles. For that reason I must say that the Leo and Capricorn match really is not one of the best combinations in the zodiac. Warm, outgoing and expressive Leo seems to be diametrically opposed to sober and realistic Capricorn.

Your ruler, the Sun makes you sunny and bright in the way you express yourself. Capricorn doesn't have quite the same ability to openly show their feelings as quickly as you. They will feel quite at odds with your dramatic and attention seeking nature. Capricorn, although independent and capable in many respects, could feel uncomfortable in your presence. You have a tendency to outshine them.

Be more sensitive to Capricorn's introverted nature. It's not that they won't open up to you but you mustn't push them. Give them time to share the depths of their personality. Capricorn is in no way a superficial individual—just somewhat mistrusting in the initial stages. Show them the way to take life a little less seriously. This more serious attitude is obviously part and parcel of their temperament so it won't be an easy job on your part to change them. Basically your temperaments are very different.

You are outward-orientated. Saturn is your complete opposite with a cooler more reflective attitude. Inward looking Capricorn is far more solitary than you and like its sister Virgo prefers to work behind the scenes. You actively seek recognition and attention. Your contrasting energies can provide some interesting times, but

LEO

only if you are both prepared to compromise and meet each other halfway. In your sexual affairs and intimacy, this contrasting difference in your expression makes it difficult for you to ever really connect physically.

Capricorns born between the 22nd of December and the 1st of January are probably too aloof and cool for you. This class of Capricorn-born individuals will express the traits of Capricorn fully and are truly represented by Saturn, the ruler of Capricorn. They are very cautious, security conscious and not usually all that spontaneous and comfortable talking about their inner feelings. You'll have your work cut out with them. Money is also very important to them.

Capricorn individuals born between the 2nd and the 10th of January are exceptions to the above sexual rule and respond to you sensually. Although the majority of Capricorns tend to be conservative in their expressions, once you get to know them you'll find that they exhibit a whole new range of emotions that you would never have anticipated.

You feel intellectually stimulated by Capricorn people born between the 11th and the 20th of January. You experience deep friendship with them as well. They possess excellent communication skills. You work together and come up with some refreshingly new financial plans that will augment your financial and future security.

LEO + AQUARIUS
Fire + Air = Hot Air

Leo and Aquarius are opposite signs of the zodiac and this can be an exciting, sometimes unusual relationship. Anything but dull and boring that's for sure. In astrology, when a star sign is in the opposite sign it's considered lucky in love and the partnership can prosper but only under certain conditions. That seems to apply with a match between Leo and Aquarius.

In some ways the Aquarian is detached much of the time and this is quite at odds with your outgoing and bubbly nature. But the two of you do have one or two things in common. You're both wilful and self-centred. You need to adjust to each other's strong personalities should you wish to develop a friendship any further.

Both of you are fixed in your opinions and find it difficult to adjust to each other's demands. From social to political and philosophical viewpoints, there will be a battle of wills that isn't easy to reconcile. One of you will have to defer or this partnership could become extremely combative. The airiness of Aquarius will inflame your fires of rage at times.

Some Leos are particularly conservative believe it or not. Aquarius is very progressive and doesn't have a lot of respect for the conventions of life. Here is another point of contention. You might start to ask yourself—is there any merit in this relationship?!

LEO

Yes. Just because someone is conventional and the other is progressive doesn't mean that they can't take a little of each other and live life in both worlds.

In the case of Leo and Aquarius you could surprisingly and unexpectedly find yourselves very attractive to each other. Aquarius is always abrupt or sudden by nature. Marriage, or at least a serious relationship heading in that direction, will be a natural consideration at some point in time after you meet. Your sexual relationship could be rather exciting believe it or not. When the Sun and Uranus combine the effect can be quite explosively enjoyable.

In looking for a secure and long-term friendship Aquarians born between the 21st and 30th of January fulfil this specific need. They are well suited to your temperament, notwithstanding some of the above quirks of nature. There's just enough of a difference to keep you on your toes and to make life a lot of fun.

You will regard Aquarians born from the 31st of January to the 8th of February as stimulating friends who wish to share their insights and experiences with you. They are also known to be good lovers so they also seem to be quite a well-suited temperament to yours.

Probably the best match with Aquarians would be with those born between the 8th and the 19th of February. You'll find them staunchly loyal supporters of anything you attempt and will therefore not

LEO + PISCES
Fire + Water = Steam

It could be because Pisceans are just so enigmatic that you need to understand them. At first it may not be the emotional or even physical attraction that draws you to them. A surreal type of curiosity could grab you hook, line and sinker. But be careful, curiosity killed the cat! You may dive into an emotional ocean in which you could drown, and never be rescued from.

Pisces is the last sign of the zodiac and is known to reflect the most intuitive, spiritual and selfless aspects of human nature. They are primarily concerned with issues of selflessness and living an idealistic type of life. As a Leo you are strongly preoccupied with the idea of doing things bigger and better, expressing your outward personality and developing your ego, both for social and material gain.

Due to these extreme differences in your nature, both of you may find it rather difficult to reconcile your very different perspectives on life and love. It will be almost impossible for you to not bring into the relationship these two vastly different viewpoints. It seems that respect and tolerance for these very different attitudes would be a fine start to commence your relationship.

LEO

There are always merits in any relationship even if the astrological assessment is not 100 per cent. Your attraction to Pisces could lead you into some unusual avenues of self-development and philosophical interest. You'll soon understand that Pisces works on a completely different level, often not revealing much of their world. Their means of communicating is also very different and you will have to adapt yourself to this non verbal form of expression.

They, in turn, will be able to reciprocate some not so obvious benefits that will eventually become valuable assets in your search for professional and personal success. The emotional and sexual energies between the two of you are most unusual but by the same token don't necessarily work all that easily. Pisces will arouse you but you need to allow yourself the opportunity to experience love and sex from a different angle with them.

The difficult Pisces individual for you is born between the 19th and the 28/29th of February. There may be an initial sexual attraction between you but the financial and practical parts of your life will not be altogether compatible.

Pisceans born between the 1st and the 10th of March reveal a slightly more sensitive and responsive side to their personality. You like this responsive aspect as you won't be left in the lurch wondering exactly what is on their minds. A lot of Pisces have a tendency to daydream and not clearly articulate where their minds are wandering.

STAR SIGN COMPATIBILITY

There are some exceptions to the above guidelines I have given you and if you choose a relationship with a Pisces born between the 11th and the 20th of March you might find that they have a little more fire in them than you ordinarily expect to find in Pisces-born lovers. There is an element of Scorpio in their make-up making them extremely passionate and loving.

2011:
The Year Ahead

LEO

2011: THE YEAR AHEAD

Live out of your imagination, not your history

—Stephen Covey

Romance and friendship

2011 offers Leo important challenges romantically which, if met head-on with a positive attitude, will result in a tremendous growth spurt and wonderful new experiences.

You can't push things however. In January, as the year commences, Mars and Saturn slow things down, cause you to feel frustrated that you're not able to achieve the emotional results that you desperately desire.

Communication is particularly stifled by this right-angled position of Mars and Saturn. Fortunately, when Venus transits your zone of romance on the 7th, things should start to improve but may still not take off as quickly as you'd like.

For this reason, the Moon and Mercury hint at humour and goodwill being the most notable tools or weapons in your fight against these obstacles.

You also have an incredible amount of sensual and sexual energy, due to the close proximity of Jupiter and Uranus. Jupiter has been transiting your zone of sexuality, transformation and shared resources for some time but now this energy can be explosive. You want to deepen your relationships and may feel thwarted because your partner, spouse or lover may not be reciprocating in exactly the way that you want. Patience, Leo!

LEO

You continue to be idealistic about life, social engagements and other romantic affairs. This is due to the transit of Neptune, the most idealistic and spiritual zone of the zodiac, transiting your zone of marriage. It will continue to be in this place for sometime and in January, be careful not to see your relationships through rose-coloured glasses. Take them off and relate to your loved ones in a practical way. In this manner you won't be disappointed by building things up to unrealistic heights.

February should be a much more engaging and fulfilling time with Mercury entering your marital zone on the 3rd. This brings you speed of communication, quick results and also with the Sun and Mars activating your partnerships, your discussions will be anything but boring. One point, however, is that you must listen a little more than you speak as misinterpretations are likely during this phase.

By the 20th, some disputes or misunderstandings may get out of hand, this again has something to do with the rapidity of your speech or a temporary inability to listen to the other person's viewpoint.

March is one of the better months for Leo with Venus bringing a tremendous amount of charm and attractiveness to your life. This can work both ways with Venus initiating a desire to improve your looks, to enhance your cultural aptitude, manners and general day-to-day living habits to improve your friendships and personal interactions.

Karmic planets influence your zone of love affairs, children and creativity after the 2nd. You have some brilliant flashes of insight which can be converted into creative opportunities. In this sphere of activity, there are ample opportunities to meet new people, forge new friendships and shift your focus towards meaningful heart/soul connections. For some born under Leo, the karmic path may change now and a whole new direction can be taken.

During the end of April and early May, a sudden surge of desire may overtake you. This is a period when the norm will bore you. You will want a change of pace, activities that enliven your zest for life and you will more than likely reach out to others who are a little different to yourself. Extending your hand in friendship will be met with enthusiasm and therefore you shouldn't be afraid of strangers or those who seem a little outside your normal gamut of social activity. Your social and emotional education continues very strongly during the month of May.

Poetry, music and other activities that stimulate your soul are spotlighted this month as well, and news or letter writing, due to the combination of Mercury and Jupiter, will fascinate you. Returning to the written word gives you an opportunity to put your thoughts and your feelings on paper and to connect with or clarify the sum of your relationships.

Friendships are on the go after the second week of June, with Venus bringing loads of fun and jam-packed activities with your normal peer group. There'll be news of some of your best friends finding love in

LEO

their lives. Goodwill on your part, even if you haven't yet met your soulmate, is an assurance of good karma coming back to you.

Communications clear up this month due to the direct movement of Saturn in your zone of communications. Any misunderstandings can now be resolved.

Mars also enters your zone of friendships after the 21st. Avoid arguments with friends—live and let live. You can't expect everyone to think the same way as you.

It's time for a pause throughout late June and early July. Avail yourself of an opportunity to step off the treadmill and recharge your batteries. You may have an opportunity to do this with someone close but my advice is to spend a little time alone during this period to reappraise your friendships and relationships—familial, romantic and social.

A new love affair may spark your interest throughout July but there are complications associated with this person—either that of culture, circumstance or morality. Ask deeper questions to get to the bottom of this person's status. You don't want to throw yourself head over heels into a relationship only to find later that it's inappropriate.

You can't expect your words or others assurances to go exactly to plan throughout August. Mercury's retrogression on the 3rd is usually an indicator of insufficient information or a change in plans when you least expect it. Diarise everything clearly; get people to confirm appointment times and you also, yourself, should be clear and concise in conveying any ideas or directives. You could be accused of getting it all wrong and confusing issues.

There can be a new addition to your family after the 21st when Venus enters your second zone of material gains, family profits and pleasure. News of an engagement or marriage could thrill you. If you're single, you might be saying, 'If only it was me.' Don't lose heart, Leo, the year's not over yet.

You might find it just a little difficult getting into the swing of your friendships throughout September. This is due to the reverse movement of Jupiter. Just remember that if others change their mind on you, you mustn't overreact, and that often this is the seed of better things happening to you. You may feel a little bit down, unappreciated or disconnected from your usual group of friends. Once again you may need to go out on your own and explore life without the crutch of others being there to support you all the time. This is a very strengthening exercise and can serve to broaden your horizons in life generally. Don't let your moods get the better of you.

You are quite serious in October but not in a bad way. Mercury conjoins Saturn as Venus transits your zone of family, parents and inner happiness and contentment. You're likely to be a little bit more focussed, and concentrated on what needs to be done at home to remove emotional handicaps from your life. This is all good but don't forget it takes two

LEO

to tango and you may need to deal with those who are not yet prepared to clear the air, let go of past grievances and start afresh.

In November, Venus and Mercury return to your zone of romance, love and children. For those of you who are married, your relationship with kids can be reactivated and you'll discover the inner child within yourself as a result. Playing games, sport, taking up a hobby or simply exploring some new avenues to enrich your life will give you a great deal of joy. Doing this with your children if you're a parent will help in the bonding process and enhance your experience of parenthood.

Finally, as December comes around, take care of your emotional health and your health and wellbeing generally. If you're out partying, take precautions if you are active in that way (if you know what I mean). You need to maintain hygiene and also optimum dietary and lifestyle practices to remain on top of your game. Clear eyes are far more attractive to the opposite sex.

A lunar eclipse in your zone of friendships this month highlights the need to revisit the issue of friendships, their value in your life and whether or not you're wasting your time with some people. You'll need to be ruthless in weeding out those who no longer provide you any value. At first you could be upset about this process but in the long run, especially as you move into 2012, you'll realise the benefits that can come to you as a result of this. Creating space to attract new people into your life is the name of the game as 2011 winds down.

Work and money

You're committed to achieving your goals throughout 2011 but overwork is a distinct possibility which could result in a lowered vitality, difficult health issues and therefore a less productive beginning to the year.

Mars, the Sun, and Pluto, posited in your sixth zone of daily work routine, indicate a heavy dose of energy which needs to be managed properly in January. By directing your energies in a healthy way, resting adequately and not trying to cram too much work into a short space of time, you'll be in a better position to enjoy the benefits of your work as well as good health and happiness, particularly throughout February and March.

Throughout March and April there will be issues surrounding your finances that need to be worked out and let me tell you, there's no point sweeping these factors under the rug. There have been challenges throughout the previous twelve months that need to be addressed now. If you have debts, mortgages or other payment schedules that are falling behind, this is the time to get on top of it, plan a budget and stick to it. Even if you need to enlist the help of a third party, it's a good opportunity to do so and get real clarity over your financial affairs as the year commences.

Your career planet is Venus. This is the prin-

LEO

cipal power associated with your success in life and at once tells you that you need to use tact and charm to achieve the best results. Venus is fast moving throughout March and April, reaching your zone of ethics and legalities in the early part of April. You need to sort out contractual issues with employers, educate yourself to improve your skills professionally and/or possibly even travel for your work.

During May, when Venus climbs to the pinnacle of your horoscope, around the 15th, you have a perfect opportunity to achieve something notable in your professional line. You'll be popular, able to influence others, including your superiors.

The other incredible astrological factor that we can't overlook throughout June and July is the entry of Jupiter, the supreme benefice and excellent karmic planet for Leo, entering your zone of profession.

Jupiter's influence will remain with you for approximately one year, so this is most certainly the time to create your business plan, set up new goals and objectives and to make some resolutions towards which you should actively direct your energies. No doubt, success is yours and if not, it's only a matter of time, with it being just around the corner. Get ready to meet your destiny.

Mars is powerful in giving you an increased income during July. In fact, Mars has a strong association with some of your past karma and this could even indicate some lost or unclaimed moneys coming to light. Check all your receipts, your commission state-

2011: THE YEAR AHEAD

ments and pay checks. For some of you, a pay rise that has been delayed may come all at once, offering you some additional funds to play with. Enjoy.

You can't be too cautious in August, with Mercury in retrogression. Contracts should be checked and then re-checked again with someone else acting as a mediator. I can't tell you the number of times I've seen people impulsively sign on the dotted line only to find out later that they were completely misinformed and enthusiastic for the wrong reasons. Always read the fine print during this sort of cycle.

You're quick with money and able to grasp some new opportunities in September. Mercury enters into the vital earning zone of your horoscope and underpins the fact that you will be talking finance, thinking and possibly even living and breathing money. There could be a lot at stake, which is why when quick-moving planets like Mercury pass through this part of your horoscope, you need to be doubly sure that your calculations are correct and that you don't cut corners.

Another factor here is Mars entering your Sun zone around the 19th of September. This makes you arrogant, aggressive and determined to make you get what you want, when you want, irrespective of the damage that you may cause. Tread lightly and remember that a soft, quietly assertive nature is just as effective, sometimes more, than loud and rambunctious demands.

You can speculate in November but speculation

LEO

is an awful lot like gambling, so don't do it if you haven't researched it or taken the time to practice beforehand. Many fools throw away their money, arrogantly thinking that they have all the answers and can win a million dollars on the stock market. I have been advising many of my clients since 2001 to invest in gold. During this period the value of this commodity has risen 200 per cent, being the ruling metal for Leo. Don't rush into this, but do investigate this precious metal as a potential form of long-term security.

As I said earlier, with Jupiter positively moving through your zone of career and self-esteem, this should be one of the best periods professionally for 12 years. Make the most of it.

Karma, luck and meditation

The luckiest planet for Leo is Jupiter. As it moves in the upper part of your horoscope, you'll be surprised at how easily some things will come to you.

Your past karma is indicated by its journey through your nineth zone of previous good deeds and this should have already been quite well noted by you as it has been there in your nineth zone for some time. Jupiter will however move to your powerful tenth zone of career and self-identity on the 4th of June, highlighting a shift to a more outward phase in which you can make some great inroads into your professional life. You'll be received well, should achieve a better position in life generally and should overall find happiness as

2011: THE YEAR AHEAD

Jupiter influences your fourth zone of family, inner contentment and also finances.

Health and vitality should be enhanced through Jupiter's entry into this upper part of your horoscope. So I also foresee a lot of luck in health problems diminishing and even difficult and stubborn conditions being relieved after the middle part of the year. Thank you Jupiter.

Venus, although not quite as beneficial to you, is still considered a first-rate provider of good luck, particularly in the area of romance, love and relationships. We see that this planet can offer you some excellent friendships, introductions and windows of opportunity when it transits through the eleventh zone of life fulfilment after the 9th of June. Other periods, when Venus may also provide you with exceptional opportunities are the end of July and November, when it transits your zone of love affairs.

Interestingly, Venus also makes a last minute arrival into your zone of marriage on the 20th of December. This signifies a thoroughly satisfactory end to 2011 with romance being one of your greatest luck factors during this final leg of the year. Good luck in your love, work and life generally!

LEO

Your Bonus 2010 Three Month Forecast

OCTOBER 2010

Highlights of the month

This is a busy month. What you have to do may not feel comfortable and you prefer to hide away from the world for a while. Unfortunately that's not going to work and, with the Sun combining with Saturn in your zone of communications around the 1st, you have to stand up and tackle your problems head on. In addition, others may not be so accommodating to your needs and you'll be tested in your social skills and diplomacy.

My prediction is you'll pass through this time with flying colours, as long as you don't react too strongly to others' judgements of you. They may have a misconception of who you are and what your motivations might be. This is a common problem but here you will be one step ahead of the crowd.

You'll be asked to help solve some riddle or problem this month, as evidenced by Mercury moving through your zone of thinking. The task may be a difficult one but you'll be up to it after

LEO

the 5th, so accept the challenge. This may be one of those periods when the pay-off is not necessarily monetary but your good name will be enhanced as a result and your reputation can grow. Over and above this, you'll enjoy the challenge of resolving an issue to both your own and any other's satisfaction.

If you're involved in sales or public speaking, then when touring, teaching or in any other sort of negotiation, you'll be extremely clear and articulate in the way you present your case. Sales agents will be lucky enough to earn better commissions and longer-term contracts. Your journeys will also be fruitful and you mustn't complain if your work or a client expects you to travel further than you would normally expect to. You'll gain extra unasked-for benefits.

Studying for your work is also on the cards throughout October and, although you'll have to put in some extra hours to learn the topics, it will no doubt help you develop greater skills that you can apply in your workplace now or in some future employment. Educational matters are spotlighted between the 21st and the 23rd.

If you're sitting through examinations or something like them, you'll be ready to take the test by the 28th when your mind and power of concentration will be supercharged. I expect you to come out on top with excellent results, irrespective of the arena in which you are being tested.

Romance and friendship

You may be desperate to improve your social status between the 4th and the 6th, but you mustn't appear to be trying too hard. Understand that the planets will give you the emotional support you need. One point, however: During this cycle, you mustn't take friendships for granted. People can only bear so much and remember that giving as well as taking is part and parcel of true friendship.

The period of the 8th to the 12th will bring you considerable sexual tension and/or excitement in your relationships. Working on your boundaries will be a fairly important component of how well your relationships work. If something doesn't feel right, draw a line in the sand.

Between the 13th and the 15th, you can smooth over many of your tensions and your lover will now be more agreeable. You're also likely to be unconditional in the way you express your love.

While this is one of the major secrets of a fulfilling love life, my strong suggestion for you between the 16th and the 19th is that you now keep a thorough control over any highly passionate impulses. You may need to keep your cards a little closer to your chest rather than speaking openly about what you want. This will give you a strategic edge in your relationships. 'Silence is golden' and gives you the upper hand.

There are some unexpected events domestically between the 23rd and the 29th. Someone in your family circle may get up and leave quite unexpectedly. If you're a parent with children in their late teens or early twenties, you may need to talk some sense into them before they throw all cares to the wind.

Work and money

Between the 3rd and the 9th you have to be beyond reproach if you're going to lecture others. Your personal habits and belief systems could come into question if you're expecting others to behave in a certain way. This is one case where the statement 'do as I say and not as I do' is an inadequate argument.

You could be caught off guard if you're looking at investing and overhauling your finances between the 11th and the 15th. You mustn't listen to the layperson who is a supposed 'expert'. Because you yourself haven't got the requisite knowledge, you might assume that their jargon is a reflection of some deeper wisdom, which isn't necessarily the case.

You'll be excited to learn about some new methods to 'up the ante' with your earnings, but please be careful of treading on the toes of others when doing so. It's fine being all fired up about sharing your vision of wealth and success with your friends but, if you overdo it, you could start to annoy them.

I see considerable extravagance around you after the 28th. There's no use spending all your hard-earned cash only to find yourself back to square one economically. Continue to be moderate in your spending and don't throw bad money after good simply to make an impression on others.

Destiny dates

Positive: 21, 22

Negative: 12, 24, 25, 26, 27, 29

Mixed: 3, 4, 5, 6, 7, 8, 9, 10, 11, 13, 14, 15, 16, 17, 18, 19, 23, 28

NOVEMBER 2010

Highlights of the month

Your mind could be off with the fairies, so to speak, in the first few days of the month, so try to pay more attention to what other people are saying otherwise you'll miss some crucial advice or direction.

During the period of the 1st till the 4th you may be invited somewhere only to find yourself lost on the way. Allow additional time to study your directory or better still get yourself a satellite navigation system in your car. They're not that expensive and will save you a lot of time, especially if you've got a somewhat poor sense of direction.

Nervous tension to do with your savings, taxes and other investment portfolios will cause you to lose sleep and be distracted from other important work this month. Speculations after the 9th are likely to be done in haste and this is ill-advised. You may be listening to the wrong people when it comes to making a quick buck. Remember that unless you carefully analyse the markets and study business

2010: NOVEMBER

and investments diligently, you are as good as gambling.

Jupiter's combination with Uranus can throw a spanner in the works with a surprise announcement by your spouse or a business partner around the 19th or 20th. It is far preferable to have your own bank account than rely on other people's financial arrangements. If you're at the mercy of what's happening somewhere else, you'll never be totally financially independent. Now is the time to turn that around. Make some decisive steps towards taking full control of your own financial situation.

If a plan backfires now, you've only got yourself to blame. You may have been taking your eye off the ball, while others have been running with it. Why would you then be surprised if the rules of engagement change as well? Still, you do have a say, and probably have a little more control than you think you do.

If some of these issues are still lingering from a domestic fallout several months earlier, your negotiation skills will require a reasonable amount of sweetener to make the cup palatable to others. Try to be nice when demanding what you believe is a fair deal for all concerned. It may just work for you.

If your children are at an age where they are likely to want freedom and independence because they are adults, this is a time where one of them may leave your domestic situation. What is known as the empty nest syndrome could now be encountered and needs to be dealt with.

LEO

Between the 28th and the 30th, take the time to talk to your children about their plans so that you're not completely bowled over when, out of the blue, they decide to pack their bags and leave.

Romance and friendship

There may be irritating social obligations between the 4th and the 8th. Someone might put the hard word on you and you'll have no choice but to sacrifice your time, energy and—hopefully not money—to fulfil their demands.

From the 9th till the 13th, friendship and love are spotlighted and will give you considerable satisfaction. Because of the presence of Venus, your physical looks and charm will play an increasingly larger role in attracting all sorts of people to you. Don't let your ego get the better of you, but of course it's okay to soak up just a little bit of adulation.

Expect lots of fun times and enjoyable pastimes from the 14th to the 20th. You'll find yourself in the company of those who are like-minded. It's also a cycle in which your artistic endeavours will prosper and, should you choose to take up some sort of artistic or creative activity, you'll feel very comfortable channelling your energies.

From the 22nd to the 24th there's a wonderful opportunity for you to hook up with an unusual group of people in some sort of social event that is not a run-of-the-mill situation. If this is apart from your usual peer group, it's probably best to keep

2010: NOVEMBER

the details of it a secret or you may be ridiculed for trying something so different.

Travel urges are growing from the 25th to the 29th, so it's not a bad time to get out your brochures and make some firm plans. Someone from a foreign place could befriend you and this could trigger your interest in different cultures.

Around the 30th exciting affairs could eventuate and you need to seize the opportunity quickly enough, otherwise you could regret having been too slow off the mark.

Work and money

It's a great feeling, having the appreciation and respect of those you work with and for. This is most likely your experience between the 1st and the 5th because your mental brilliance will captivate the imagination of others. They will feel inspired by you, which gives you the opportunity to prove your abilities as a leader, even if it's only a temporary position.

Networking your skills provides many opportunities in your career between the 10th and the 19th. Some gathering or a social event may be a key to opening new doors in your professional life. Dress to the max and put your best foot forward.

Decisions that have been hanging in limbo can move forward after the 12th. Having the correct facts at your fingertips helps communications. You have more confidence to speak your mind, knowing that you can back up what you say with the correct data.

A comfortable period at work awaits you between the 20th and the 24th. A get-together with co-workers and family members to show your successes of the year is likely, and this should be a special time where connections between work and family are harmonious.

Destiny dates

Positive: 9, 10, 11, 12, 13, 14, 15, 16, 17, 18, 21, 22, 23, 24, 25, 26, 27

Negative: 6, 7, 8

Mixed: 1, 2, 3, 4, 5, 19, 20, 28, 29, 30

DECEMBER 2010

Highlights of the month

In this last month of the year, you would think that fun, Christmas cheer and other festive activities would dominate your life, wouldn't you, but this couldn't be further from the truth. In fact, there may be more work around than you had anticipated, so clear the decks and be prepared to roll up your sleeves and get into it, at least until the 10th. You may have no choice because several of your work colleagues may decide to disappear early, leaving you to shoulder the additional workload.

Mercury's retrogression late in the year indicates you might have overlooked a few jobs or deadlines only to find that you're having to play catch-up between the 12th and the 18th. Part of the problem may have been your interpretation of the directions given to you by your manager. Slacking off will not exclude you from the extra hours you will have to put in now to level the playing field. There's no use

LEO

ignoring the prevailing issue or trying to postpone fixing it till after Christmas. You'll only feel irritated and won't enjoy your Christmas dinner. My advice is: better to do it now and get it out of the way.

You should expect at least one blow up prior to Christmas Day and the most likely timing of that—from what I see in your horoscope—is the period of the 14th till the 19th, when Mercury and Pluto conjoin. You could be grilled by someone who has no real authority and you could retaliate, creating some bad blood in the process. Work could be a sensitive issue and the people you're dealing with may be just as strung out as you are. Try to remain empathetic about this fact and no harm will come to you.

Watch your health around the 20th, leading up to Christmas. Don't go rushing headlong into things; give yourself ample time and, if you are unclear about the way to do something, don't be too proud to ask for assistance. You're likely to hurt yourself or possibly damage some apparatus, computer technology or other machinery. Read the instructions!

There is a final lunar eclipse on the 21st of December, which takes place in your zone of friendships. This is the final movement in the Leo forecast for 2010 and it hints at the fact that much of your satisfaction in the last couple of weeks of the year will hinge upon the successful communication you will have with friends. As burdened as you will now be by your workload, accommodate a friend's call for help. It won't erode too much of your own valuable time but it will go a long way towards cementing your bonds of friendship with this person.

Romance and friendship

From the 2nd to the 5th, don't let your high level of energy cause unexpected mishaps or injuries. It's best to move a little more slowly and think about your actions before you begin them.

From the 7th to the 10th, your long-term romantic plans may have to be postponed and this might be upsetting, especially if you'd looked forward to an engagement or even a wedding date. However, don't let these turn of events throw your life into chaos. There will be a good reason for what's happening: the universe has a mind of its own and you will benefit from working harmoniously with this idea. Keep an open, positive mind that things will work out for the better.

Between the 16th and the 19th, an unusual situation arising with a friendship might start to lead to feelings of romance. This may be particularly tricky if you happen to work with this individual. The situation could be confusing when, after having developed an attitude of professionalism together, you find you now have a much deeper sense of connectedness with them. Explore the relationship by all means, but don't let it ruin your workplace ethics.

Your sports and physical pastimes are high on the agenda between the 20th and the 25th. This is a

LEO

time to explore new hobbies and outdoor activities with which you can combine your social life. Don't forget the added benefit of renewing your health and re-invigorating your mental and emotional faculties.

The period of the 28th till the 30th could be a testing cycle for you when your philosophy, religion or belief systems will be put to the test. You need to prove that you have the courage of your convictions or people may consider you to be the great pretender. You'll be thoroughly scrutinised by your peers, so it's better to say as little as possible.

Work and money

Pay more attention to your letter writing skills and the means by which you communicate between the 1st and the 4th. Communication devices may need to be tested thoroughly, possibly even upgraded. Use your perks at work to save yourself money by putting it on the professional bill.

A desire to improve your lifestyle may force you to reconsider some of your financial obligations and whether or not you can afford such a change. Industry and consumer magazines can be helpful in this respect and will give you good comparisons based upon price and quality. This is likely to be strongly highlighted between the 12th and the 18th.

Focus your attention on something that's unique after the 20th; something that reflects who you really are as a person. Don't be scared to work hard

2010: DECEMBER

to get a plan up and running and then stick to it, irrespective of what others might think. Of course, keep it light-hearted and don't forget to add a touch of humour to everything you do leading up to Christmas.

Courage and earnestness are the key words after the 23rd. Use grit and determination to make some valuable contributions to your workplace and your community. Social work, donations and other charitable activities have karmic financial benefits.

Destiny dates

Positive: 21, 22, 23, 24, 25
Negative: 1, 2, 3, 4, 5, 7, 8, 9, 10, 28, 29, 30
Mixed: 12, 13, 14, 15, 16, 17, 18, 19, 20

LEO

2011:
Month by Month Predictions

JANUARY 2011

Don't aim for success if you want it; just do what you love and believe in, and it will come naturally

—David Frost

Highlights of the month

Your heart is on fun things this month, however Mars, the Sun, Pluto and the karmic node all point to the fact that hard work is going to have to take precedence, especially between the 1st and the 5th.

Sometime around the 6th or 7th, your romantic life may be in for a surge of energy. Jupiter and Uranus provide you with some titillating sexual activity and this is the time when you should nurture your lover, and be nurtured. The period of the 7th till the 13th is a powerful time of bonding, forging new relationships and strengthening the bonds of love in your existing partnerships.

Health matters come to the fore after the 14th. There may be some problems you have been experiencing that are not easily deciphered. Doctors and

LEO

clinical practitioners may have a hard time figuring out what, if anything is wrong. You may start to feel as if you're a little bit crazy, but this could all stem from an excessive workload, emotional stress and also continual worry over imaginary problems. The solution to this may be more metaphysical than physical.

Meditation, spiritual practices, deep breathing and other forms of physical exercise may be the simple short cut to increasing your health and well-being this month.

Between the 18th and the 20th you will be detective-like in your research. You can apply the energies of Mercury and Pluto to gaining valuable information that is hidden or not easily accessible by the masses. You can also focus your attention on some niggling work problem that is not easily solved. Using unconventional means to resolve issues is the way to go.

The Sun enters your zone of marriage, business partnerships and people generally around the 20th. During this time you can create some sort of new path with someone who has a considerable amount of information or possibly even money to bring to the table. Partnerships are favoured just now, but you must also be careful not to get too excited before understanding more about them.

After the 22nd Jupiter and Saturn indicate powerful communications and new learning experiences. There are issues surrounding a sibling or possibly even neighbours which must not be postponed. Goodwill,

2011: JANUARY

courtesy and other friendly gestures may be met with resistance at this time. Mars and Saturn also challenge you to be patient and not expect a resolution to these issues too quickly.

Romance and friendship

The 1st to the 4th is a perfect time to throw all your creative energies into getting your act together at home. You need to dare to be different but also forget about distracting yourself with other external matters. By sorting out some of your domestic issues at this time, you will feel freer to enjoy what's coming in the following weeks.

A more loving energy is forecast for you between the 5th and the 8th. Take the time to share your dreams with the one you love and in the same way get them to express their feelings a little more openly.

A short journey is on the cards with the one you love or perhaps with a close friend around the 12th. If you haven't completed all your tasks, however, you may feel worried and perhaps will not enjoy your time away. Tie up any loose odds and ends before embarking on a trip away.

Friendships are tight between the 15th and the 16th but some scandalous information around the 17th could punch a hole in your bliss factor. Don't get drawn into rumours or innuendoes.

You have to do someone else's dirty work around the 22nd. Before getting embroiled in another

LEO

person's problems you should get clarity prior to making the commitment.

You are somewhat down in the dumps between the 25th and the 28th. Try not to think too much about the past. Today is a new day and the future much rosier.

Your creative impulses are again strong and love and romance are highlighted between the 29th and the 30th. On the 31st you feel ready to embark on some new friendship.

Work and money

If you are burning the midnight oil, working late and trying to meet deadlines between the 1st and the 5th, you will realise by the 8th that you need to slow down and take stock of things. It's not how much you work but how efficient you are with the time at your disposal.

Look carefully at the fine print on the 10th. If you are dealing with contracts, schedules and other time factors, you may overlook some important information which could cause problems for you around the 13th.

Time out is necessary between the 17th and the 20th. Don't be afraid to ask for some rostered time off especially if you need to regroup your energies.

Travel, intense communications and a frenetic schedule between the 23rd and the 25th are indicated. Plan your work accordingly and don't take on too many additional tasks.

2011: JANUARY

After the 26th home affairs are high on your agenda and you may need to spend some time working around the home and spending money on tasks that have been swept to the side.

A creative surge around the 28th gives you the opportunity to beautify your home, spend time in the garden or if finances allow it, to hire someone such as a landscape artist to improve your home and living space.

Destiny dates

Positive: 6, 7, 9, 11, 13, 15, 16, 18, 19, 20
Negative: 14, 27, 29, 30, 31
Mixed: 1, 2, 3, 4, 5, 8, 10, 12, 17, 22, 23, 24, 25, 26, 28

FEBRUARY 2011

Highlights of the month

Negotiation will get you everywhere this month as Mercury gives you a dose of the gift of the gab, particularly after the 3rd. You can discuss your needs and gain some leverage in these negotiations. And when Venus enters your zone of work after the 4th, part of these discussions may centre around beautifying your work environment, cleaning up mess and generally giving yourself a much better environment in which to work, rest and play.

Mars and the Sun inject you with tremendous physical drive around the 5th. Do you have an adequate outlet, however, is the question? If you're bottling up your feelings and not using this energy or directing it in a way that is constructive, you could get angry and may meet further resistance from those who would normally support you in your endeavours. Don't use brute force to get your way. Diplomacy must be employed at every step of the way up until the 13th.

2011: FEBRUARY

Around the 14th till the 20th you may become obsessed by love, or rather should I say by someone. Be careful, Leo. These obsessions may peak very quickly only to leave you in a ditch after the amorous affair is over. Take things slowly and use the power of Pluto to understand others in a deeper way rather than superficially. Understand also that some of what you may see may not be pleasing to your mind, but remember that we all have our good and bad sides and that this is only human.

You are particularly charming but also idealistic from the 17th up until the 20th. Don't allow your ideals and reality to remain too far from each other. Being grounded is essential this month if you are to make decisions that foster security and long-term relationships.

During this few days, the Sun and also Mercury heighten your responses, make you prone to being possessive, jealous and pointing the finger at someone, all out of a very reactionary state of mind. Be proactive, not reactive during these fiery days.

You'll find it difficult materialising some of your dreams between the 21st and the 23rd, but you mustn't delude yourself over what's possible, nor must you defeat yourself by thinking that things are impossible. It's all a matter of keeping a realistic tone to your living circumstances and your ambitions. Planning will be a key factor to just how easily and speedily you will achieve your goals.

Mercury enters the eighth zone of transformation during the last few days of February. Spend

LEO

some time analysing yourself. This is a deep and psychological aspect that can give you a strong sense of self-understanding. That being the case, you will be in a better position to understand how others perceive you and thereby can act in accordance with other people's plans and ambitions. This offers you the chance to further your relationships, both professionally and personally.

Romance and friendship

There are occasions when people, friends and even lovers are deceptive but from the 1st to the 3rd it could be you who is deceiving yourself. During this period, however, you will be attracted to members of the opposite sex and want a new relationship to take off. By the 4th however, when the moon conjoins Mars you could be impulsive so try to use better judgement in your choice of friends.

You are vital, interested in getting physically active and perhaps rejoining the gym after the 7th. This will make you feel good about yourself and by the 9th your self-esteem will hit a mini peak.

Friendships abound between the 11th and the 14th but you may also find yourself at odds with someone you usually get on well with especially around the 13th. Rather than seeing the differences try to find common ground and you will therefore continue to maintain good relations with that person.

You need to get someone to commit to a promise around the 19th. Words are cheap and you may feel as if you are being strung along by someone at this

2011: FEBRUARY

time. Make that difficult call or confront a person on the 20th. You may be a little emotional but at least your honesty will make a point.

Between the 21st and the 23rd there is potential to clear the air by speaking your mind but your buoyant and palpable energy will also precipitate disputes and disagreements. You probably won't worry as long as you can get things off your chest.

Meeting people in an enjoyable environment between the 26th and the 28th will foster some new styles in communication which will broaden your horizons generally.

Work and money

Don't argue about money between the 4th and the 6th. Sudden upheavals or unexpected expenses could have you or your partner pointing the finger at each other. Join hands and heads to come to a common solution that is agreeable to both of you.

Between the 11th and the 14th you may misplace some valuables or could overspend. Don't let fast talking salesmen talk you out of your hard-earned cash.

You need to be fully trusting of the people you work with particularly if you are in a business which involves a partnership. You could feel as though something is not quite right between the 17th and the 22nd. Keep your eye on the ball and if need be, investigate the issue more deeply to give yourself peace of mind.

LEO

Accounting practices and the way you manage your money are highlighted between the 21st and the 23rd. A speculative venture may be more emotional than practically based between the 24th and the 26th. Don't throw good money after bad.

You will be worried about vague work issues between the 27th and the 28th. If you can't quite pinpoint what the issue is forget it until things become clearer.

Destiny dates

Positive: 7, 9

Negative: 1, 2, 3, 13

Mixed: 4, 5, 6, 11, 12, 14, 15, 16, 17, 18, 19, 20, 21, 22, 23, 24, 25, 26, 27, 28

MARCH 2011

Highlights of the month

If you're worried about money, having sleepless nights or feeling as if you're short-changed in a relationship, particularly where it comes to finances and the resources that you share with some other meaningful person in your life, then I'll have to put it to you that you're more than likely focussing on the wrong thing.

Money is just the superficial expression of some deeper values. Money is only a part of an equation relating to your time, effort and love. Perhaps you should be focussing on the time, the effort or the love in this equation rather than the money which is the end result. In other words, the questions I would have for you between the 1st and the 8th would be, 'Are you utilising your time efficiently? Are you bringing the right sort of energy to the work or your relationship?' and most importantly of all, in all your endeavours, ask yourself whether or not you truly love in a passionate way what you're doing. If

LEO

you said, 'Yes, I love what I'm doing, I bring a lot of pure energy to my activities and I am using my time wisely,' then my additional query would be, 'Why are you worried about money?' Money will naturally flow through to you through this process.

But it's not that simple. The positions of Uranus, Mercury and the Sun as well as Mars hint at the fact that your value system may be out of step with someone else during this month. How you earn money and how you want to spend it may be at odds with how your lover or partner or even friends may choose to spend their money. Open discussion is necessary and you need to listen as much as you speak.

Uranus transits into the sign of Aries which relates to your philosophical and educational pursuits. This happens on the 21st. Some unusual interests will arise and this could suddenly make you feel as if you need to educate yourself more. Learning new things, investigating new opportunities or skills will fascinate you just now. You may even meet someone whom you admire due to their having achieved something that you also aspire to. Please don't be afraid of asking them their advice help you on your path to achieving your ideals as well.

Some sort of journey may quickly be decided upon in the last few days of the month, and this too is a result of Uranus transiting into your zone of journeys. Don't rush things however, and if you can't get the appropriate flights, accommodation

2011: MARCH

or pricing, it's best to wait, especially seeing as Mercury goes retrograde on the 30th.

Mercury's retrogression indicates that you may hastily embark upon some course of action only to find yourself in a state of regret later. You can, however, settle things up until the 27th or 28th without too much trouble. If you can't get it together before then, or someone else is playing havoc with your time or schedule, postpone these affairs until a more appropriate time.

Romance and friendship

Coupled with the previous sentiment and ethereal vibrations of these two planets, your sexual energies are also at a peak and, particularly between the 3rd and the 6th, you will be feeling rather hot and driven to express yourself physically. The combination of Mercury and Uranus also make you very clever and inventive in the bedroom.

You will be a little annoyed after the 11th when a friend tries to pry into your business. You need to give them the cold shoulder and maintain a greater degree of secrecy around your personal affairs at this time.

Losing sleep over someone or some event is quite likely between the 13th and the 15th. You mustn't dwell unnecessarily on past issues particularly if you have no control over changing those matters just now. Bide your time and when possible raise the issue and try to resolve it amicably.

LEO

Between the 16th and the 20th there are forces at work that pull the rug from under your feet but not necessarily in a bad way. An unexpected invitation, a journey or chance meeting could really enlighten you and bring you some exciting opportunities socially. Don't procrastinate as by the 21st there may be more pressing matters at home that you need to deal with.

Relationships with children may be contentious between the 25th and the 27th. Adjusting yourself to newspeak, different ways of looking at pop culture and fashion may be an eye opener but go with the flow.

Venus enters your zone of sexuality, deeper emotional connections and personal transformation after the 28th. Until the 31st you will be focussed primarily on these issues in your closest one on one relationships. There may also be some friend who needs your help and if you choose to offer advice, try to remain unbiased.

Work and money

If in the previous couple of months you took the time to set up a comfortable working environment for yourself, the 1st to the 3rd should run smoothly and you will be less cluttered in your work area. If that is not the case, you could find yourself putting out bushfires during this short interval.

Between the 6th and the 12th you need to make some resolution which will assist you in achieving some short-term goals. Try to develop an alliance with someone who can help share the workload at this time and your objectives will be reached much quicker.

Around the 17th make sure that you have enough cash on you. You don't want to find yourself in an embarrassing situation having left your valuables at home.

Between the 20th and the 25th look after work safety. Don't leave loose ends lying around that can be detrimental to you or others.

You can either reinvest the interest or returns on savings or spend them after the 27th. If you can sacrifice a little now, the interest you earn on your savings will help accelerate the growth of your assets. It's all up to you.

Destiny dates

Positive: 9, 10, 12, 16, 18, 19, 28, 29, 30, 31

Negative: 13, 14, 15, 26

Mixed: 1, 2, 3, 4, 5, 6, 7, 8, 11, 17, 20, 21, 22, 23, 24, 25, 27

APRIL 2011

Highlights of the month

What's the point of arguing with someone if their opinion is so different to yours and what's more, they won't listen to what you have to say, even if what you're offering makes so much sense. This is your plight between the 1st and the 4th. Someone (someone you probably love, too) may not see eye to eye with you. Strangely, they may agree, but remember this, it may simply be to keep the peace, not necessarily because you've convinced them of your particular perspective.

This is the time of the year when the Sun, the ruling planet for Leo, transits the upper part of the horoscope. What this signifies is the pinnacle of success, occupational opportunities and other great accolades and opportunities. For those of you who are ambitious to achieve a new position, this is the time to take an interview, throw your hat in the ring for a new post or a new job as you're likely to be successful.

2011: APRIL

Venus brings with it some beautiful energy after the 21st when it transits through your nineth zone of long-distance travel. There could well be someone who shows an interest in you, not simply for how you look but for who you are and what you believe. Connecting with someone's heart and mind may bring you a new experience of love based on a deeper respect rather than the usual conventional superficialities that go into making up your typical relationship.

This could excite you and if the person doesn't live locally, may inspire either you or them to travel for you to meet and get to know each other better.

Internet experiences, online dating and other modern forms of romance are also spotlighted during this phase of Venus's transit for Leos.

Around the 23rd some sudden meeting or opportunity of a romantic nature may find you emotionally elated but also rather nervous. This could take you out of your comfort zone as Venus and Uranus operate in an abrupt, aggressive and rather strange way.

Question whomever you meet at this time and don't assume that appearances reflect who the person really is. In the same manner, you must be completely above board about who you are and what your intentions are. You're likely to be zany, witty and desirous of some unusual experiences which may border on the fantastic. Remember: your behaviour has repercussions not just for you but for others in your life.

LEO

Mercury's direct movement after the 23rd is an excellent omen for resuming negotiations and any discussions which have stalled. Speak your mind and once you have all the facts to your liking, feel free to move forward on a handshake or a signature on the dotted line.

Romance and friendship

From the 2nd to the 5th you have a particularly strong sense of doing things differently but those you love, especially if they are conformists will try to force unpalatable methods upon you. You need to remain open to what they are presenting even if your first impression is that this is not going to be fun or it's going to be boring. Openness is your key word during this particular cycle.

Between the 12th and the 16th your plans could be somewhat up in the air. There is nothing worse than waiting for confirmation on an appointment or some directive only to find that you have either been forgotten or that others are too busy to respectfully and courteously give you the right indicators. It's always wise to have a plan B just in case you are stood up.

Put some limits on your relationships and your own tongue between the 19th and the 21st. You will be running in high gear and likely to be saying and doing things that evoke poor behaviour from others as well. Try to set up some parameters and get your friends, spouse or partner to agree to these terms. You and another person will need to short circuit a potentially heated situation.

You can achieve a more balanced approach in your relationships and friendships but from the 22nd to the 24th you will need to be more courageous and confident if you are to achieve that. There are changes in your mental wiring just now and although circumstances don't normally rattle you, internally if you are honest with yourself, you are sometimes fazed a little. This period allows you to take full control of your inner as well as your outer life and relationships.

From the 27th to the 30th a fancy dress or otherwise zany party may be the highlight of the end of your month.

Work and money

Mars, your lucky planet indicates successful resolutions to legal complications between the 2nd and the 9th. Your legal representatives can only work with the information that you give them so try to be detailed and organised in preparing the facts and figures for them.

Your nervousness will show between the 10th and the 12th. If you are attending a meeting, part of the trick is practising your delivery and overcoming stage fright. Practice makes perfect.

It may be a better idea to lock up valuables off site rather than within the home from the 14th till the 18th. Perhaps consider opening a bank safe deposit box for wills, valuable jewellery and other

LEO

important documents that can easily be misplaced in the domestic arena.

A misunderstanding or disagreement in your workplace with a co-worker or possibly even your boss can be resolved after the 23rd. All is well that ends well.

You may have some brilliant commercial or professional ideas after the 27th but around the 30th make sure that you are able to decipher your dreams and visions so that others can practically grasp what you are trying to say.

Destiny dates

Positive: 22, 23, 24, 27, 28, 29, 30

Negative: 1, 10, 11, 18

Mixed: 2, 3, 4, 5, 6, 7, 8, 9, 12, 13, 14, 15, 16, 17, 19, 20, 21

MAY 2011

Highlights of the month

You want to do things in a bigger and better way than ever due to the combined influence of Mars and Jupiter. You are thinking of faraway places, ambitions which ordinary mortals may think are unattainable. You yourself may have thought that some of these goals were previously unattainable but for some reason now the expansive qualities of Jupiter give you a sense of confidence and support as well.

Between the 1st and the 8th you have a great sense of timing. You'll find yourself in the right place at just the right time and even strangers, people you thought have no impact on your life, may suddenly connect with you, offering opportunities in work, socially and otherwise.

The dominant power of Mars enters your career zone after the 11th. Although you have enough drive to achieve a lot of work, the way you work may get your co-workers offside. Try to balance your needs

LEO

with the needs of others. Teamwork is essential and of course if you act in too domineering a fashion, you'll only alienate those who could otherwise help you get to your goals faster.

The most excellent combination of Venus and Jupiter takes place during May and offers you gifts, love and sustenance between the 12th and the 15th. You may want to lavish someone you love with gifts as a token of your appreciation for them and vice versa. Romance, new relationships or a chance meeting may appear to be like a gift from heaven just now.

Your karmic planets are moving in retrogression and this can indicate a meeting with someone from your past or perhaps a soulmate that you recognise instantly. You must be impressive in your speech without being too loud. You must be able to tell a good story without embellishing it to the extent that it makes you seem as if you're exaggerating or coming across like a braggart.

By the 22nd you'll be in receipt of some extra money which, as a result of your good efforts, will be well deserved. New friends also come into the picture at this time and an introduction into a new circle of individuals can open your eyes to some potential activities, hobbies or other activities that will spice up your life.

Jupiter continues to give you good fortune and also rekindles your desire to investigate your spiritual heritage.

2011: MAY

Romance and friendship

It's not just a matter of feeling self-confident, Leo, but also valuing yourself in the correct way. During the first few days of the month and particularly between the 1st and the 5th, you need to draw a line in the sand if a friend has taken you for granted. You have possibly been holding in a lot of feelings and not retaliating, thinking that this person's behaviour would change. While it's time to speak your mind you mustn't let them interrupt when you read them the riot act.

Between the 9th and the 11th you are lucky and your communication can have a favourable impact on others. You receive some good news during this period which will further increase your self confidence and sense of personal worth.

You are flighty between the 13th and the 15th. Try to be clear in what you want from others or you will receive mixed signals and then further confuse yourself.

Words of love, encouragement and more could make you feel wonderful around the 16th. The position of Mercury and Venus hint at a true revival of love and inner beauty. The more you share this the more you will receive in return.

From the 19th to the 21st you may be avoiding that deep and meaningful talk with a relative. Address the issue head on and get it out of the way.

Someone who hasn't been exactly above board with you may return with their tail between their

LEO

legs asking for forgiveness. From the 24th till the 29th you need to carefully examine the pros and cons of this relationship and determine whether you want them back in your life.

Work and money

If you are engaged in any sort of competitive sport or sport related field, you could be successful between the 1st and the 4th. Hard work pays off just now especially for those of you who are keen to make sport or some sideline hobby a means of earning money.

Your profitability depends upon your capability. You realise this after the 5th. Up until the 11th you find yourself in a position to discuss, negotiate and secure some additional income if you want. There are even home based businesses for those of you that are home-makers that can also add a few extra dollars to your bank account each week. Explore the possibilities.

Investments take pride of place on your agenda from the 17th until the 19th. Diversify your portfolio if what we are talking about is the stock market.

Renegotiate the terms of your agreement in a business partnership around the 22nd. Avoid passionate or overt emotional displays, positive or negative, between the 23rd and the 25th. It won't help your case commercially.

Obsolescence, and necessity are the mother of invention causing you to change some of your bad work habits between the 29th and 31st. Purchasing a new computer or some other technical apparatus to help you fast track your work is also indicated.

Destiny dates

Positive: 6, 7, 8, 9, 10, 11, 12, 16, 17, 18, 22, 30, 31

Negative: 23

Mixed: 1, 2, 3, 4, 5, 13, 14, 15, 19, 20, 21, 24, 25, 26, 27, 28

JUNE 2011

Highlights of the month

You continue to become very focussed on your professional activities. For those of you who are not professionally employed, take heart. I don't only make these references to those of you who are employed by someone, but also in respect of the work you do at home, particularly if you are homemakers and domesticated in your day-to-day life. What I'm trying to say is that between the 1st and the 5th, you'll be particularly conscious of improving your skills, perfecting your work and doing something that you can be proud of.

The solar eclipse which occurs in your zone of financial profits also is very revealing, especially if you run an independent business and want to gain insights into how to increase the profitability of your venture. You must maintain an open mind, listen to the newspeak, and expand your operations to include new technologies.

Research and development may also be necessary due to Neptune's transit into your eighth pass of discoveries. You have a greater ability than you yet suspect and must shine the torch of your creative concentration on areas that you may have overlooked in the past. All of this will give you access to new resources and new outcomes which can only benefit you creatively and financially.

This would have to be one of the most significant months for Leo. I say this due to the important angular transit of Jupiter into your career house for the first time in twelve years. For many of you this will be the completion of a cycle which of course heralds the beginning of new things. But you must also learn to let go and say goodbye when things have exceeded their use-by date.

The excellent transit of Jupiter making a favourable aspect to Pluto, the transformative planet of the zodiac, transiting your zone of work, also supports my forecast that many things will change for you in the next twelve months, beginning around this time.

A couple of other factors stand out in June and one is the fact that Venus and Mars occupy your career zone as well. A romance in the workplace is certainly not out of the question, but you know where that can lead you? Do take care and try to maintain some sort of boundary between work and pleasure.

Mercury enters the secretive twelfth house around the 16th, heralding some unsavoury news, gossip or rumours which may be unpleasant and even directed at you. Your real test at this time is how you respond to accusations and innuendo.

The problem with these sorts of energies is that if you respond by retaliating too strongly, people assume that the rumours on the grapevine may indeed be true. As this twelfth zone is a quiet, low-key and secretive area of the zodiac, my best advice would be to remain silent and to not respond at all. You need to maintain your integrity and your reputation.

Romance and friendship

There could be a strong feeling of nostalgia and a desire to return to some old friendship or state of affairs but you will know that that's not possible between the 1st and the 3rd. Accept the fact that change is ultimately for the best and that some of the people in your life may have to pursue their own path just as you do.

A state of emotional impoverishment between the 4th and the 6th is not something you should dwell on but rather look to what the benefits in your current lifestyle are. Perhaps you have become too dependent on someone and this is the cause of these feelings.

You are oscillating between extreme highs and lows from the 9th to the 12th. Fluctuating like this is not going to allow you to find the happy medium especially if you are undecided about a course which you must take in your life. Find the middle ground and weigh up the pluses and the minuses before making a decision.

You may need to be conspicuously absent from your social circle between the 14th and the 16th and this is one sure-fire way of making people miss you and appreciate who you are.

You may need to decline circulating at some social event between the 17th and the 20th for fear that someone you don't get on well with may be there. You have my full permission to reject the invitation.

Just around the 25th or 26th you may need to withdraw from a situation and this will be based purely on your insight. You can take a supreme jump from where you are to where you want to be and leapfrog some of the people who are holding you back. This may even relate to family members.

Work and money

Dealing with the fringe dwellers of society is never easy and you may find someone who envies you in your workplace around the 2nd or the 3rd. You need to act like the favourable feminist if you are a woman. If you are a male, just for safe measure carry the baseball bat in your back pocket. You may not need to use it but at least if people see it they know that you mean business.

You have to be a little subversive between the 15th and the 18th. This means working in solitude and finding out things that may not be in the public domain so to speak.

LEO

You are either in or out on the 21st. You mustn't agree to do something under pressure between the 21st and the 24th. You will only upset yourself and not create good work. Your heart needs to be in what you are doing just now.

If the opportunity presents itself why not take up the offer to do a weekend seminar and enjoying the change of scenery and the people that you will be interacting with. This is likely between the 28th and the 30th.

Destiny dates

Positive: 1, 14, 15, 28, 29, 30

Negative: 6, 21, 22, 23, 24

Mixed: 2, 3, 4, 5, 9, 10, 11, 12, 16, 17, 18, 19, 20, 25, 26

JULY 2011

Highlights of the month

It's a fun-filled month as indicated by the transit of Mercury into your Sun sign. You'll definitely feel better, even from the 1st. Notwithstanding the solar eclipse in your twelfth zone of secrets; you'll still feel good about yourself. Perhaps you throw up some stuff from the past and are able to deal with it, and remove it.

From the 4th till the 12th I see a great deal of expenditure. This is not a bad thing, because you'll thoroughly enjoy the experience of a little retail therapy. But why not do this: when you're spending your money look at art objects or other items which over time may acquire value rather than throwing your money away haphazardly. There's spending and then there's spending. Intelligent spending means that what you buy may in due course become more valuable over time.

Here's a case in point: I have a friend, a famous musician who has a house full of guitars. Many of

LEO

these guitars he bought 20 or 30 years ago for a song in little second-hand shops. There's one there now that I know of which is worth at least $20,000. He probably only spent a few hundred dollars on that at the time. So, like that, if you must spend, spend your money wisely.

Sleepless nights may be your lot after the 23rd. What's bothering you? It may not even be anything you can pinpoint. Mars, along with one of your karmic planets, can sometimes indicate disturbances in your energy field not caused by the usual sort of day-to-day worries. Utilise spiritual techniques to heal and align yourself.

After the 28th, Venus enters your Sun sign. What a stroke of luck! Venus is all attractive and promises a wonderful new makeover, new hairstyle, fashion, fabrics and other items of luxury that can be used to beautify and enhance your personality. I've noted that some people under this transit, particularly if Mars is involved, might want to engage in some cosmetic surgery to enhance their facial features.

You don't have to go that far, but you could well experiment with different colours, tones and shades to create a new 'you'. In any case, these last few days of the month are an excellent self-pampering time where you can devote a little bit of attention to yourself and pat yourself on the back for a job well done.

Romance and friendship

Good news can sometimes be a little daunting even if you feel blessed when you hear what's on offer. With success comes additional responsibility. News that someone is interested in you or has accepted you more openly also means that you may have to restrict or curtail some of your activities to make yourself available for them. From the 2nd to the 7th try not to put all your eggs in one basket just in case the outcome is not exactly as you had imagined.

Think much more deeply about your emotional needs particularly when the Moon moves to the fifth zone of love affairs after the 13th. Up until the 15th you should gather up your resources and reconnect with those people who can help make things happen and who also have perhaps some added insights to add to your own to improve matters.

The Moon and Jupiter combine on the 23rd bringing to your doorstep some unforseen benefits. You may also meet someone that you wish to help without any thought of reward. Your compassionate feelings are strong and there is a strong spiritual flavour to the energies surrounding this particular injunction.

On the 28th you have an opportunity to dominate your social landscape but you should do this in a diplomatic fashion where you can lead others and remind them of their own power as well. The sharing of power in your social circumstances will be spotlighted.

LEO

Don't forget that you may somehow overlook someone's birthday or an important annual date. Around the 30th be sure you have pencilled into your diary all the birth dates of those that mean something to you. A little forethought will spare you any emotional turmoil or embarrassment later.

Work and money

You will be extremely busy but if you are ill-prepared a lot of stress can be associated with your activities and up until the 7th you should try to be a step ahead of those that you are working with or more importantly in competition with. A more detailed and organised approach will decompress your stress considerably.

Gather up all the resources you need between the 13th and the 18th. You need as much ammunition as possible to finetune your strategy. If you haven't been delegating sufficiently, that could be part of the problem as to why you are not able to complete your tasks on time and you are feeling depleted of energy. Get others to give you a hand with what needs to be done at work or at home.

If you are in a position of control in your workplace you must allow others to attempt something which is ridiculous and possibly far-fetched from the 20th till the 25th. You may at first recoil and wonder what's going on but stepping away from the norm is how new techniques, new strategies and even products and inventions are developed. Give your underlings the opportunity to prove themselves.

Destiny dates
Positive: 1, 7, 13, 14, 15, 16, 17, 18, 28
Negative: 8, 9, 10, 11, 12
Mixed: 2, 3, 4, 5, 6, 7, 20, 21, 22, 23, 24, 25, 30

AUGUST 2011

Highlights of the month

Mercury is once again retrograde this month and asking you to hold off making important decisions which would ordinarily not be too big a deal excepting for the fact that the month commences shortly after a new moon.

A new moon indicates that you want to create a new you, embark upon new beginnings, a fresh start and so on and so forth. With Mercury retrogressing, you may be halted in your stops and may well find yourself having to postpone some new venture or business plan as well. This may be the third time I've mentioned it for your forecast but patience, dear Leo.

On the one hand, you may know what you should and want to do, but may be obstructed if someone doesn't readily agree to your words of advice. What can you do? You can't twist people's arms and you must realise that each man or woman's destiny is ultimately in their hands.

2011: AUGUST

At this point in the game you'll hopefully realise that acceptance is an important component in living life in the company of other humans. We may try to change things but often we have very little or no control over it. These transits in your horoscope during the first part of August may lead you to question these issues more deeply.

There's a better quality of energy after the 16th but here again the Sun and Venus in conjunction may create some problems for your spouse or lover. This combination is called combustion. Venus becomes weak under the rays of the Sun and likewise, someone close to you may be overworked, irritable and incapable of reciprocating the love that you so desire.

Unconditionally giving to them may be the only hope you have of keeping the relationship on an even keel. This may be difficult because you yourself may feel needy and don't understand why the person in question isn't able to supply your needs.

Between the 21st and the 26th you may be the recipient of some unasked for gift, money or advice. Venus is a blessing to you at this point, and moves into a slightly better phase, having passed its square aspect to Jupiter. Around the 23rd the Sun will also combine, bringing focus again on monetary matters.

Although Mercury goes direct on the 26th, allowing you the ability to finalise some plan or contract, Jupiter in retrogression means that you

LEO

may still have to postpone or wait for the final nod from someone in a superior position.

Romance and friendship

As the Sun and Venus occupy your sun sign of Leo at the outset of the month you will feel as if you are on cloud nine. Making new connections is on the cards between the 1st and the 4th and it's likely some of the turmoil you have seen in your personal relationships is likely to subside due to Mars' exit from your zone of friendships at this time.

Communications are much more solid from the 3rd till the 7th. A seductive interlude around the 5th, a passionate encounter either with someone known or not so well known is probably the start of many more similar encounters after this.

Around the 15th till the 20th you may have a difficult choice between two people. This could be divided loyalties between two friends or possibly even two potential lovers. Making decisions based on appraising one character against another is not an easy thing. There is no rush as long as you are honest and let others know you are undecided.

You may hear news of some old long-term friends of the family after the 23rd. This will rekindle many memories and there is even the possibility that you have a chance to meet up with them in pleasant circumstances.

Between the 21st and the 25th you could be accused of not giving enough attention to your nearest and dearest. It's hard juggling work, relationships and family demands and it could simply be a matter of you wanting to spend a little time away and not deal with these issues.

Play along with a practical joke after the 28th. You could easily find yourself feeling embarrassed by something someone says or does in a situation that makes you feel rather like a fish out of water. Try to see the humour in the situation.

Work and money

Because you are prepared to confront some of your financial situations and fears, the period of the 1st till the 6th can be an eye-opener and will remove a lot of the confusion surrounding money. This is an excellent period to remove blockages in your finances.

A friend or younger member of the family may need some assistance financially between the 8th and the 12th. Sometimes money is not the solution but rather helping someone to help themselves. Look at the best case scenario for them rather than just handing money over and teach them the skills to earn and manage money for themselves.

Some people can talk a great story but you need to be careful between the 15th and the 18th. You may be hoodwinked into believing that you can somehow make a lot of money by circumventing the usual processes. If something sounds a little too good to be true it probably is.

LEO

An impulse purchase made between the 26th and the 29th may be done for the wrong reasons. Keeping up with the Joneses is never a good motivator. If you need something buy it but if it is simply to save face or play games of one-upmanship, you are mistaken.

Destiny dates

Positive: 1, 2, 3, 4, 5, 6, 7

Negative: 27, 29

Mixed: 8, 9, 10, 11, 12, 15, 16, 17, 18, 19, 20, 21, 22, 23, 24, 25, 26, 28

SEPTEMBER 2011

Highlights of the month

People may be getting you down and that could be their way of thwarting your happiness. Between the 1st and the 5th, try not to pay too much attention to that negativity around you. If you feel that you're absorbing too much of the negative emotions of the people that you work or live with, get out. Spend time alone if you have to, and revitalise yourself near a river, sit at the beach, walk through bush and re-oxygenate that brain of yours. This is the way to overcome these bad vibrations.

Speaking of getting out, the most notable transit this month is that of Venus into your house of short journeys. Mobility, travel and simply getting away from your normal routine will be a pleasure. Your work may also bring you more travelling, more activity and communication with the world around you. In any case, it might appear a coincidence but will be timely, just as the people around you are trying to bring you down.

LEO

On the 19th, Mars activates you Sun sign. Be careful, though, Leo. You already have an abundance of power, vitality and energy. Mars only serves to turn the heat up on an already heated up system. Channelling your energies now is of vital importance. Ordinarily I would say that you'll be able to direct this power in a constructive manner, but by the same token you may be a little insensitive to others who are not quite as wound up as you.

Remain aware of the needs of others and engage them, invite them to join you in this exciting phase of your life. This is a time to lift others up, not just yourself. Especially when you have an abundance of this Martian energy.

You may receive some communication after the 23rd that stops you dead in your tracks. This could be news from a friend or a family member that is not easily digested. It can affect the quality of your routine and may anger you, especially if what is requested is at a moment's notice, leaving you little or no time to reschedule other appointments and important engagements. There are times when these sorts of things are unavoidable and you may simply have to take some time out, reorganising your diary for this specific issue.

By the 29th Venus and Saturn create a cooling effect on your life. The traditional meaning of this combination of energies is one of sobering up. Your passions may wane and you may wonder what more lays in store for you, as far as your love life is concerned. Especially if you're feeling that it is

2011: SEPTEMBER

a little bit tedious and uneventful. It's up to you to create some interest in your partner and do something that will re-engage them in the relationship. You can do it.

Romance and friendship

There could be a few days, notably between the 1st and the 4th when you mean well, you want to express your feelings so deeply but somehow the translation between heart and head gets lost. What then comes out of your mouth can be completely misconstrued leaving you feeling out on a limb. In these situations it's far better to say less than necessary.

Be on guard for wolves in sheep's clothing between the 8th and the 13th. If you wait until the 14th, you will understand what I am saying here.

Inoculate yourself against cynical humour around the 15th. People aren't trying to have a dig at you but you may be overly sensitive and could overreact to some of their harmless statements.

Between the 16th and the 18th your state of being satisfied will depend upon your mutual interaction with friends and those who can fulfil your needs as much as you can theirs. Saturate yourself with good feelings but make sure the other person is prepared to reciprocate as well.

Having a preconceived idea about someone is not necessarily bad but you may need to keep things to yourself between the 19th and the 22nd.

LEO

Fully appraise the situation before forming a firm opinion.

Between the 23rd and the 25th try to preserve the peace. If you can do so this will be a memorable time and could involve you visiting someone whom you initially didn't believe would be as entertaining as they end up being.

Be careful to dress appropriately between the 27th and the 29th. You don't necessarily have to go overboard with your makeup, fashion and other accessories to make a lasting impression. You could be tempted to dress a little too young for your age thereby inviting criticism.

Work and money

The combining of your resources and skills with someone else in your workplace between the 1st and the 5th is the way to surmount some challenging circumstances at work. Don't play the 'I am an island unto myself' game as this will thwart your efforts.

Either you will be re-examining your work or someone will be examining you between the 6th and the 10th. This may not be simply a cursory glance at what you are doing but a microscopic, micromanaging of your affairs. Are you up to the task of passing the grade? Prepare.

You should despise the free lunch and never remain indebted to anyone else. Usually if someone is offering something and you feel uneasy about it, rest assured payback will come around if not immediately then at some time in the future. Between the 12th and the 16th pay your own way.

Opportunities to acquire property that has gone under the hammer of the bank such as foreclosures, give you the perfect chance to get your new home, if that's what you have been planning. Make the appropriate enquiries and don't feel too guilty about gaining an advantage through someone else's misfortune. This is all part of the karmic wheel of life.

Destiny dates

Positive: 17, 18, 19, 20, 21, 22, 24, 25

Negative: 11

Mixed: 1, 2, 3, 4, 5, 6, 7, 8, 9, 10, 12, 13, 14, 15, 16, 23, 27, 28, 29

OCTOBER 2011

Highlights of the month

Thank God you're clear and methodical in your thinking processes during October. Between the 1st and the 5th you won't easily allow emotion to take over your sensibilities. This is good because if you've been feeling a little put out in some sort of relationship, you'll be able to think beyond the moment and your reactions such as doing and saying something that can't be taken back.

After the 6th you'll feel better about things as Venus enters your zone of family affairs on the 9th. This is an excellent time to focus your attention on family, relatives, your personal history and your own inner fulfilment. You'll be able to create a safe haven at home and will be able to take more interest in the value of family life and the ones you cherish.

If you've been way too social, it's easy to neglect the ones that have stood by you through thick and thin. Feeling sentimental and experiencing more appreciation for what you have will most likely arise.

2011: OCTOBER

On this point, the attitude of gratitude is an important philosophical component and will also be useful in combating feelings of negativity, lack, and other problems with your perspective on life.

Going closer to women in your life, the softer, more feminine energies of nature are likely to be aroused in you as Venus winds its way through this most important angular zone of your horoscope.

This feeling should intensify when Mercury moves through the same zone on the 13th. Greater communication is likely, even with relatives that have been out of the picture for sometime. There are also some issues surrounding vehicles, transportation and other machinery. You may buy a new car at this time or consider overhauling the one that you have. Think carefully about this as once you've purchased something like a brand new vehicle, it can lose value very rapidly.

Physical, active energies surrounding these matters come to the fore after the 23rd when the Sun enters your fourth zone of family. Demolishing walls, repainting, stripping back, doing the gardening and other landscape or structural changes to your home can all take place under this transit.

Work may take a back seat just now as the Sun, your vital, ruling planet enters the lower part of the zodiac. Don't resist this as the planets also have their seasons and demand that you become aware of what needs to be done during these times.

LEO

Relax, spend time with friends and family in a cloistered domestic environment and withdraw yourself to build up your reserves of energy. This will ultimately provide you additional fuel with which to come back into the world with more vim and vigour.

Romance and friendship

Although you feel amorous between the 1st and the 5th you may not be adequately interested in sex. Your energies are more driven by intellect and emotion and so you need to be on the same page as your partner during this phase. Talk about your feelings.

Go shopping for that engagement or wedding ring if your relationship has reached fullness at this point in time. Venus forecasts a long-term and committed relationship is probably in order just now. Excellent dates to negotiate and possibly purchase jewellery and other tokens of emotional commitment are the 6th, 8th, 10th, 13th and 16th.

Don't let being late to a party ruin your evening after the 18th. You can still enjoy yourself even if you don't spend quite as much time as you would have liked in the company of others.

Don't forget to take your camera with you on the 20th or 21st. Take some snapshots to memorialise the event or situation even if it happens to be very casual. You will take great pleasure in what eventuates and can express yourself artistically.

2011: OCTOBER

From the 22nd till the 24th you are forceful and your willpower is strong. You are able to make a promise and give expressions and assurances but others may not be quite as prepared to do so. You must engage them and get them to undertake the same sort of level of commitment as yourself.

To clean and polish a surface you sometimes need to produce a friction by rubbing, smoothing, cleaning and polishing. Your relationships are the same and this may be the case between the 28th and 31st. Don't be afraid of friction particularly if it can bring out the best in your love affair at this time.

Work and money

Between the 3rd and the 9th you have to be beyond reproach if you're going to lecture others. Your personal habits and belief systems could come into question if you're expecting others to behave in a certain way. This is a case of 'doing as I say and not as I do' being an inadequate argument.

You could be caught off guard if you're looking at investing and overhauling your finances between the 11th and the 15th. You mustn't listen to the layman who is a supposed 'expert'. Because you yourself haven't got the requisite knowledge, you might assume that the jargon is a reflection of some deeper wisdom. That isn't necessarily so.

You'll be excited about some new methods to up the ante with your earnings but please be careful in treading on the toes of others in doing so. It's fine

LEO

being all fired up about sharing your vision of wealth and success with your friends but if you overdo it, you could start to annoy them.

I see considerable extravagance around you after the 28th. There's no use spending all your hard-earned cash, only to find yourself back to square one economically. Continue to be moderate in your spending and don't throw bad money after good simply to make an impression on others.

Destiny dates

Positive: 8, 9, 10, 11, 12, 13, 16, 20, 21, 22, 23, 24, 26, 27

Negative: None

Mixed: 1, 2, 3, 4, 5, 6, 7, 18, 28, 29, 30, 31

NOVEMBER 2011

Highlights of the month

You want love more than ever and on the 2nd when Venus and Mercury jointly move into your fifth sector of creative love affairs, you'll be lucky enough to get what you want. Now, even if you happen to be in a relationship, this is an excellent omen to kick-start your love life again. Don't play mind games, however. If you want to say, 'I love you,' do so. You'll be totally satisfied with the response that you get.

This is a time of kinship with friends but also with children. Allow the inner child in you to blossom. Generate feelings of love, compassion and fun. You need to explore love, not just talk about it. Remember, love is a verb. Act upon your feelings during this phase and the universe will reciprocate. What goes around comes around. Remember, that's the law of karma.

By cushioning yourself with love, joy and a fresh outlook you'll be better able to weather the storm of the Sun/Saturn conjunction on the 13th. This brings

LEO

with it additional responsibilities that may not be easy. But the metal in the hands of the blacksmith only becomes tough, useful, if it's beaten, placed in the fire, then the water, and beaten again on the anvil.

Remember that life's blows and all the challenges that confront you are nature's way of strengthening you as well, my friend.

There's nothing worse than fighting about money or material goods. Unfortunately, Mars's entry into your zone of money on the 11th is not particularly a favourable omen. There may be misunderstandings with friends or family members.

Service is a particularly important key word this month. Later in the month, when Venus transits your sixth zone of work and service on the 26th, you may feel as if everyone is demanding more of you than they can justify. Once again your resistance to these life forces is what will be the cause of problems, not the fact that people are indeed demanding. An open-hearted response will diminish your resistance and pain, and will in fact give you a strong sense of fulfilment, usefulness and joy.

Don't cut corners either, but go the extra mile and see how it feels. Venus, if you recall, is an artistic planet, creative by nature and therefore you can apply these principles to any problem, rather than using your brain with maximum, positive results. Finally, if your partner or lover feels isolated this month, compassionately talk to them, or rather listen to what they have to say and make them feel better. This too is a fine type of service.

Romance and friendship

There may be irritating social obligations between the 4th and the 8th. Someone might put the hard word on you and you'll have no choice but to sacrifice your time, energy but hopefully not money, to fulfil their demands.

From the 9th till the 13th, friendship and love are spotlighted and will give you a lot of satisfaction. Because of Venus, your physical looks and charm will play an increasingly larger role in attracting all sorts of people to you. Don't let the ego get the better of you, but it's okay to soak up just a little bit of adulation.

Expect lots of fun times and enjoyable pastimes from the 14th to the 20th. You'll find yourself in the company of those who are like-minded. It's also a cycle under which your artistic endeavours will prosper and should you choose to take up some sort of artistic and creative activity, you'll feel very comfortable channelling your energies.

From the 22nd to the 24th, there's a wonderful opportunity for you to hook-up with an unusual group of people in some sort of social event that is not your run-of-the-mill situation. If this is apart from your usual peer group, it's probably better to keep the details of this secret or you may be ridiculed for trying something so different.

Travel urges are growing from the 25th to the 29th so it's not a bad time to get out your travel brochures and make some firm plans. Someone

LEO

from a foreign place could befriend you and this could trigger your interest in different cultures.

After the 30th exciting affairs could eventuate and you need to seize the opportunity quickly enough, otherwise you will regret having been too slow off the mark.

Work and money

It's a great feeling, having the appreciation and respect of those you work with and for. This is most likely between the 1st and the 5th as your mental brilliance will captivate the imagination of others. They will feel inspired by you and this gives you the opportunity to prove your abilities as a leader, even if it's only a temporary position.

Networking your skills provides many opportunities for you in your career between the 10th and the 19th. Some gathering at a social event may be a key to opening new doors in your professional life. Dress to the max and put your best foot forward.

Decisions which have been hanging in limbo can move forward after the 12th. Having the correct facts at your fingertips helps communications. You have more confidence to speak your mind, knowing that you can back up what you say with the correct data.

A comfortable period at work awaits you between the 20th and the 24th. A get-together with co-workers and family members to show your successes of the year is likely, and this should be a special time where connections between work and family are harmonious.

Destiny dates

Positive: 8, 9

Negative: 1, 11, 12, 28, 29, 30

Mixed: 2, 3, 4, 5, 6, 7, 13, 14, 15, 16, 17, 18, 22, 23, 24, 25, 26, 27

DECEMBER 2011

Highlights of the month

You're a person on a mission this month with Venus entering the orb of Pluto. You are committed to achieving your goals but Venus of course relates to relationships and love and therefore you may be pushing too hard to get a response. Did you know that many of the physical problems that we experience have an emotional basis? This is one such time that you should pay close attention to my words and remember what I'm saying here as this can have a very powerful impact on your general wellbeing.

If you're emotionally dissatisfied and trying to push someone to their limits to satisfy your own needs, it won't work. It will, in fact, backfire. Rather, I would say, why not use the glorious energies of Mercury and the Sun in the fifth zone of your horoscope to lighten things up a little. Laugh a little. You can use satire and a little bit of quirky cynicism to get your point across, rather than being totally serious. That should do the trick.

2011: DECEMBER

You're on the pulse culturally throughout December and between the 6th and the 10th you may exhibit some interest in something quirky in society. There may be some new trend or some opening for you to jump on the bandwagon. This may have more to do with a work or creative activity but it's certainly something that should be investigated.

There's a technical theme surrounding this astrological component and therefore don't be afraid to look into emerging technologies and how these can possibly be used in tandem with the work that you do. You need to move with the times.

This is the last month of the year and as I mentioned in the yearly overview, the entry of Venus into your marital sector is a wonderful note to complete 2011 on. There may be late proposals, engagements, and wedding invitations or perhaps some final fulfilment or desire granted from the one that you love. In any case, this transit is exceptionally friendly and loving so I'd say that after the 20th, much of what you've been aspiring to throughout the year, particularly with reference to love, is likely to come to fruition, if not fully, at least to a larger extent.

Jupiter, in its direct motion on the 25th, Christmas Day, is also an excellent omen, promising a new twelve year phase of expansion, growth, spiritual insight and worldly fulfilment as well. May the stars shine upon you and bring you happiness and love throughout the coming weeks and months!

Romance and friendship

From the 2nd to the 5th don't let your high level of energy cause unexpected mishaps or injuries. It's best to move a little more slowly and think about your actions before you actually begin them.

From the 7th to the 10th, your long-term romantic plans may have to be postponed and this might be upsetting, especially if you'd looked forward to an engagement or wedding date. There's good reason for this, the universe has a mind of its own and you need to work harmoniously with that. Don't let this throw your life into chaos. Keep an open, positive mind that things will work out for the better.

Between the 16th and the 19th, an unusual situation arising with a friendship might start to lead to feelings of romance. This may be particularly tricky if you work with this individual. It could be confusing, having developed an attitude of professionalism with them, only to find that you now have a much deeper sense of connectedness with them. Explore the relationship by all means, but don't let it ruin your workplace ethics.

Your sports and physical pastimes are high on the agenda between the 20th and the 25th. This is a time to explore new hobbies and outdoor activities with which you can combine your social life. Don't forget the added benefit of renewing your health and re-invigorating your mental and emotional faculties.

The period of the 28th till the 30th could be a testing cycle for you and your philosophy, religion

2011: DECEMBER

or belief systems will be put to the test. You need to prove that you have the courage of your convictions or otherwise, people may consider you the great pretender. You'll be thoroughly scrutinised by your peers so it's better to say as little as possible.

Work and money

Pay more attention to your letter writing skills and the means by which you communicate between the 1st and the 4th. Communication devices may need to be tested thoroughly, possibly even upgraded. Use your perks at work to save yourself money by putting it on the professional bill.

A desire to improve your lifestyle may force you to reconsider some of your financial obligations and whether or not you can afford the change. Industry and consumer magazines can be helpful in this respect and will give you a really good comparison based upon price and quality. This is likely to be strongly highlighted between the 12th and the 18th.

Focus your attention on something that's unique after the 20th, something that reflects who you really are as a person. Work hard on getting a plan going and then stick to it, irrespective of what others think. Of course, keep it light-hearted and don't forget to add a touch of humour to everything you do leading up to Christmas.

Courage and earnestness are the key words after the 23rd. Use grit and determination to make some valuable contributions to your workplace and your community. Social work and donations

LEO

and other charitable activities have karmic benefits financially.

Destiny dates

Positive: 4, 5, 6, 7, 8, 9, 10, 11, 12, 13, 14, 15, 16, 17, 18, 19, 20, 24, 25, 26, 27, 28, 29, 30, 31

Negative: 22

Mixed: 1, 2, 3

2011:
Astronumerology

LEO

2011: ASTRONUMEROLOGY

I have a simple philosophy: Fill what's empty. Empty what's full. Scratch where it itches

—Alice Roosevelt Longworth

The power behind your name

It's hard to believe that your name resonates with a numerical vibration, but it's true! By simply adding the numbers of your name, you can see which planet rules you and what effects your name will have on your life and destiny. According to the ancient Chaldean system of numerology, each number is assigned a planetary energy. Take a look at the chart below to see how each alphabetical letter is connected to a planetary energy:

AIQJY	=	1	**Sun**
BKR	=	2	**Moon**
CGLS	=	3	**Jupiter**
DMT	=	4	**Uranus**
EHNX	=	5	**Mercury**
UVW	=	6	**Venus**
OZ	=	7	**Neptune**
FP	=	8	**Saturn**
—	=	9	**Mars**

The number 9 is not allotted a letter because it is considered 'unknowable'. Once the numbers have been added, establish which single planet rules your name and personal affairs. At this point the number 9 can be used for interpretation. Do you think it's unusual that many famous actors, writers and musicians have modified their names? This is to attract luck and good fortune, which can be made easier by using the energies of a friendlier planet. Try experimenting with the table and see how new names affect you. It's so much fun, and you may even attract greater love, wealth and worldly success!

Look at the following example to work out the power of your name. A person named Andrew Brown would calculate his ruling planet by correlating each letter to a number in the table, like this:

A N D R E W B R O W N
1 5 4 2 5 6 2 2 7 6 5

Now add the numbers like this:

1 + 5 + 4 + 2 + 5 + 6 + 2 + 2 + 7 + 6 + 5 = 45

Then add 4 + 5 = 9

The ruling number of Andrew Brown's name is 9, which is ruled by Mars (see how the 9 can now be used?). Now study the name–number table to reveal the power of your name. The numbers 4 and 5 will also play a secondary role in Andrew's character and destiny, so in this case you would also study the effects of Uranus (4) and Mercury (5).

Name–number table

Your name-number	Ruling planet	Your name characteristics
1	**Sun**	Attractive personality. Magnetic charm. Superman-, superwoman-like vitality and physical energy. Incredibly active and gregarious. Enjoys outdoor activities and sports. Has friends and individuals in powerful positions. Good government connections. Intelligent, spectacular, flashy and successful. A loyal number for love and relationships.
2	**Moon**	Feminine and soft, emotional temperament. Fluctuating moods but intuitive, and possibly even clairvoyant abilities. Ingenious nature and kind-hearted expression of feelings. Loves family, mothering and home life. Night owl who probably needs more sleep. Success with the public and/or women generally.
3	**Jupiter**	Sociable, optimistic number with fortunate destiny. Attracts opportunities without too much effort. Great sense of timing. Religious or spiritual inclinations. Naturally drawn to investigate the meaning of life. Philosophical insight. Enjoys travel and to explore the world and different cultures.
4	**Uranus**	Volatile character with many peculiar aspects. Likes to experiment and test novel experiences. Forward thinking, with many extraordinary friends. Gets bored easily so needs plenty of inspiring activities. Pioneering, technological and creative. Wilful and obstinate at times. Unforeseen events in life may be positive or negative.

LEO

Your name-number	Ruling planet	Your name characteristics
5	Mercury	Sharp wit, quick thinking and with great powers of speech. Extremely active life. Always on the go, living on nervous energy. Youthful outlook and never grows old. Looks younger than actual age. Young friends and humorous disposition. Loves reading and writing. Great communicator.
6	Venus	Delightful and charming. Graceful and eye-catching personality who cherishes and nourishes friends. Very active social life. Musical or creative interests. Great moneymaking opportunities as well as numerous love affairs indicated. Career in the public eye is quite likely. Loves family but is often troubled over divided loyalties with friends.
7	Neptune	Intuitive, spiritual and self-sacrificing nature. Easily duped by those who need help. Loves to dream of life's possibilities. Has healing powers. Dreams are revealing and prophetic. Loves water and will have many journeys in life. Spiritual aspirations dominate worldly desires.
8	Saturn	Hard-working, ambitious person with slow yet certain achievements. Remarkable concentration and self-sacrifice for a chosen objective. Financially focused but generous when a person's trust is gained. Proficient in one's chosen field but is a hard taskmaster. Demands perfection and needs to relax and enjoy life.

2011: ASTRONUMEROLOGY

Your name-number	Ruling planet	Your name characteristics
9	Mars	Extraordinary physical drive, desires and ambition. Sports and outdoor activities are major keys to health. Confrontational but likes to work and play really hard. Protects and defends family, friends and territory. Individual tastes in life but also self-absorbed. Needs to listen to others' advice to gain greater successes.

Your 2011 planetary ruler

Astrology and numerology are intimately connected. As already shown, each planet rules over a number between 1 and 9. Both your name *and* your birth date are governed by planetary energies.

Simply add the numbers of your birth date and the year in question to find out which planet will control the coming year for you. Here is an example:

If you were born on the 12th of November, add the numerals 1 and 2, for your day of birth, and 1 and 1, for your month of birth, to the year in question, in this case 2011, the current year, like this:

Add 1 + 2 + 1 + 1 + 2 + 0 + 1+ 1 = 9

The planet ruling your individual karma for 2011 will be Mars because this planet rules the number 9.

You can even take your ruling name-number, as shown previously, and add it to the year in question, to throw more light on your coming personal affairs, like this:

LEO

A N D R E W B R O W N = 9
Year coming = 2011
Add 9 + 2 + 0 + 1 + 1 = 13
Add 1 + 3 = 4

This is the ruling year number, using your name-number as a basis.

Therefore, study Uranus's (number 4) influence for 2011. Enjoy!

1 is the year of the Sun

Overview

The year 2011 is the commencement of a new cycle for you. Because the Sun rules the number 1, the dominant energy for you in the coming year is solar, which is also connected to the sign of Leo. Expect the coming year to be full of great accomplishments and a high reputation regarding new plans and projects. This is the turning of a new page in the book of your life.

You will experience an uplifting of your physical energies, which makes you ready to assume fresh responsibilities in a new nine-year cycle. Whatever you begin now will surely be successful.

Your physical vitality is strong and your health should improve. If you've been suffering physical ailments, this is the time to improve your physical wellbeing because recovery will be certain.

You're a magnetic person this year, so attracting people into your life won't be difficult. Expect a

2011: ASTRONUMEROLOGY

new circle of friends and possibly even new lovers coming into your life. Get ready to be invited to many parties and different engagements. However, don't go burning the midnight oil because this will overstretch your physical powers.

Don't be too cocky with friends or employers. Maintain some humility, which will make you even more popular throughout 2011.

Love and pleasure

Because this is the commencement of a new cycle, you'll be lucky in love. The Sun also has influence over children, so your family life will also entail more responsibility. Music, art and any other creative activities will be high on your agenda and may be the source of a new romance for you.

Work

Because you are so popular and powerful this year, you won't need to exert too much effort to attract luck, money and new windows of opportunity through your work and group activities. Changes that you make professionally now will pay off, particularly in the coming couple of years. Promotions are likely and don't be surprised to see some extra money coming your way as a pay rise.

Improving your luck

Because Leo and the number 1 are your rulers this year, you'll be especially lucky without too much effort. The months of July and August, being ruled by Leo, are very lucky for you. The 1st, 8th, 15th

LEO

and 22nd hours of Sundays will be especially lucky. You may also find yourself meeting Leos and they may be able to contribute something to your good fortune throughout the coming year.

This year your lucky numbers are 1, 10, 19 and 28.

2 is the year of the Moon

Overview

The Moon represents emotional, nurturing, mothering and feminine aspects of our natures and 2011 will embody all of these traits in you, and more.

Groundbreaking opportunities in your relationships with family members can be expected. This will offer you immense satisfaction.

Your emotional and mental moods and habits should be examined. If you are reactive in your life, this year will be the perfect time to take greater control of yourself. The sign of Cancer, which is ruled by the Moon, is also very much linked to the number 2 and therefore people born under this sign may have an important role to play in your life.

Love and pleasure

Your home, family life and interpersonal relationships will be the main arenas of activity for you in 2011. You'll be able to take your relationships to a new level. If you haven't had the time to dedicate and devote yourself to the people you love, you can do so throughout the coming twelve months.

Thinking of moving? These lunar energies may cause you to change your residence or renovate your current home to make your living circumstances much more in tune with your mind and your heart.

Work

Working from home can be a great idea—or at least, spending more time alone to focus your attention on what you really want—will benefit you professionally. You need to control yourself and think carefully about how you are going to achieve your desired goals.

Women can be a source of opportunity for you and, if you're looking for a change in work, use your connections, especially feminine ones, to achieve success.

Improving your luck

The sign of Cancer being ruled by the Moon also has a connection with Mondays and therefore this will be one of your luckier days throughout 2011. The month of July is also one in which some of your dreams may come true. The 1st, 8th, 15th and 22nd hours on Mondays are successful times. Pay special attention to the new and full Moons in 2011.

The numbers 2, 11, 20, 29 and 38 are lucky for you.

3 is the year of Jupiter

Overview

Number 3 is one of the luckiest numbers, being

LEO

ruled by Jupiter. Therefore, 2011 should be an exciting and expansive year for you. The planet Jupiter and the sign of Sagittarius will dominate the affairs of your life.

Under the number 3 you'll desire a richer, deeper and broader experience of life and as a result your horizons will also be much broader. You have the ability to gain money, to increase your popularity, and to have loads of fun.

Generosity is one of the key words of the number 3 and you're likely to help others fulfil their desires, too. There is an element of humanity and self-sacrifice indicated by this number and so the more spiritual and compassionate elements of your personality will bubble to the surface. You can improve yourself as a person generally, and this is also a year when your good karma should be used unselfishly to help others as well as yourself.

Love and pleasure

Exploring the world through travel will be an important component of your social and romantic life throughout 2011. It's quite likely that, through your travels and your contacts in other places, you may meet people who will spur you on to love and romance.

You'll be a bit of a gambler in 2011 and the number 3 will make you speculative. This could mean a few false starts in the area of love, but don't be afraid to explore the signs of human possibilities. You may just meet your soulmate as a result.

If you're currently in a relationship, you can deepen your love for each other and push the relationship to new heights.

Work

This is a fortunate year for you. The year 2011 brings you opportunities and success. Your employers will listen to your ideas and accommodate your requests for extra money.

Starting a new job is likely, possibly even your own business. You will try something big and bold. Have no fear: success is on your side.

Improving your luck

As long as you don't push yourself too hard you will have a successful year. Maintain a first-class plan and stick to it. Be realistic about what you are capable of. On the 1st, 8th, 15th and 24th hours of Thursdays, your intuition will make you lucky.

Your lucky numbers this year are 3, 12, 21 and 30. March and December are lucky months. The year 2011 will bring you some unexpected surprises.

4 is the year of Uranus

Overview

Expect the unexpected in 2011. This is a year when you achieve extraordinary things but have to make serious choices between several opportunities. You need to break free of your own past self-limitations, off-load any baggage that is hindering you, in both your personal and professional lives. It's an

LEO

independent year and self-development will be important to achieving success.

Discipline is one of your key words for 2011. Maintain an orderly lifestyle, a clear-cut routine, and get more sleep. You'll gain strong momentum to fulfil yourself in each and every department of your life.

Love and pleasure

You may be dissatisfied with the current status quo in your relationships, so you're likely to break free and experiment with something different. Your relationships will be anything but dull or routine. You're looking for someone who is prepared to explore emotional and sexual landscapes.

Your social life will also be exciting and you'll meet unusual people who will open your eyes to new and fruitful activities. Spiritual and self-help activities will also capture your attention and enable you to make the most of your new friendships.

Work

The number 4 is modern, progressive and ruled by Uranus. Due to this, all sorts of technological gadgets, computing and Internet activities will play a significant role in your professional life. Move ahead with the times and upgrade your professional skills, because any new job you attempt will require it.

Work could be a little overwhelming, especially if you've not been accustomed to keeping a tight schedule. Be more efficient with your time.

2011: ASTRONUMEROLOGY

Groups are important to your work efforts this year, so utilise your friends in finding a position you desire. Listen to their advice and become more of a team player because this will be a short cut in your pathway to success.

Improving your luck

Slow your pace this year because being impulsive will only cause you to make errors and waste time. 'Patience is a virtue', but in your case, when being ruled by the number 4, patience will be even more important for you.

The 1st, 8th, 15th and 20th hours of any Saturday will be very lucky for you in 2011.

Your lucky numbers are 4, 13, 22 and 31.

5 is the year of Mercury

Overview

Owing to the rulership of 2011 by the number 5, your intellectual and communicative abilities will be at a peak. Your imagination is also greatly stimulated by Mercury and so exciting new ideas will be constantly churning in your mind.

The downside of the number 5 is its convertible nature, which means it's likely that, when crunch times come and you have to make decisions, it will be difficult to do so. Get all your information together before drawing a firm conclusion. Develop a strong will and unshakable attitude to overcome distractions.

LEO

Contracts, new job offers and other agreements also need to be studied carefully before coming to any decision. Business skills and communication are the key words for your life in 2011.

Love and pleasure

One of the contributing factors to your love life in 2011 is service. You must learn to give to your partner if you wish to receive. There may be a change in your routine and this will be necessary if you are to keep your love life exciting, fresh and alive.

You could be critical, so be careful if you are trying to correct the behaviour of others. You'll be blunt and this will alienate you from your peers. Maintain some control over your critical mind before handing out your opinions.

You are likely to become interested in beautifying yourself and looking your best.

Work

Your ideas will be at the forefront of your professional activities this year. You are fast, capable and also innovative in the way you conduct yourself in the workplace. If you need to make any serious changes, however, it is best to think twice before 'jumping out of the pan and into the fire'.

Travel will also be a big component of your working life this year, and you can expect a hectic schedule with lots of flitting about here, there and everywhere. Pace yourself.

Improving your luck

Your greatest fortune will be in communicating ideas. Don't jump from one idea to another too quickly, though, because this will dilute your success.

Listen to your body signals as well because your health is strongly governed by the number 5. Sleep well, eat sensibly and exercise regularly to rebuild your resilience and strength.

The 1st, 8th, 15th and 20th hours of Wednesdays are your luckiest, so schedule your meetings and other important social engagements at these times.

Throughout 2011 your lucky numbers are 5, 14, 23 and 32.

6 is the year of Venus

Overview

The number 6 can be summed up in one beautiful four-letter word: LOVE! Venus rules 6 and is well known for its sensual, romantic and marital overtones. The year 2011 offers you all of this and more. If you're looking for a soulmate, it's likely to happen under a 6 vibration.

This year is a period of hard work to improve your security and finances. Saving money, cutting costs and looking to your future will be important. Keep in mind that this is a year of sharing love *and* material resources.

LEO

Love and pleasure

Romance is a key feature of 2011 and, if you're currently in a relationship, you can expect it to become more fulfilling. Important karmic connections are likely during this 6 year for those of you who are not yet married or in a relationship.

Beautify yourself, get a new hairstyle, work on looking your best through improving your fashion sense, new styles of jewellery and getting out there and showing the world what you're made of. This is a year in which your social engagements result in better relationships.

Try not to overdo it, because Venus has a tendency towards excess. Moderation in all things is important in a Venus year 6.

Work

The year 2011 will stimulate your knowledge about finance and your future security. You'll be capable of cutting back expenses and learning how to stretch a dollar. There could be surplus cash this year, increased income or some additional bonuses. You'll use this money to improve your living circumstances because home life is also important under a 6 year.

Your domestic situation could also be tied in with your work. During this year of Venus, your business and social activities will overlap.

Improving your luck

Money will flow as long as you keep an open mind

2011: ASTRONUMEROLOGY

and positive attitude. Remove negative personality traits obstructing you from greater luck. Be moderate in your actions and don't focus primarily on money. Your spiritual needs also require attention.

The 1st, 8th, 15th and 20th hours on Fridays are extremely lucky for you this year and new opportunities can arise when you least expect it.

The numbers 6, 15, 24 and 33 will generally increase your luck.

7 is the year of Neptune

Overview

Under a 7 year of Neptune, your spiritual and intuitive powers peak. Although your ideals seem clearer and more spiritually orientated, others may not understand your purpose. Develop the power of your convictions to balance your inner ideals with the practical demands of life.

You must learn to let go of your past emotional issues, break through these barriers to improve your life and your relationships this year. This might require you to sever ties with some of the usual people you have become accustomed to being with, which will give you the chance to focus on your own inner needs.

Love and pleasure

Relationships may be demanding and it's at this point in your life that you'll realise you have to give something to yourself as well, not just give to others

LEO

indefinitely. If the people that matter most in your life are not reciprocating and meeting your needs, you'll have to make some important changes this year.

When it comes to helping others, pick your mark. Not everyone is deserving of the love and resources you have to offer. If you're indiscriminate, you could find yourself with egg on your face if you have been taken advantage of. Be firm, but compassionate.

Work

Compassionate work best describes 2011 under a 7 year. But the challenges of your professional life give you greater insight into yourself and the ability to see clearly what you *don't* want in your life any more. Remove what is unnecessary and this will pave the way for brighter successes.

Caring for and helping others will be important because your work will now bring you to a point where you realise that selfishness, money and security are not the only important things in life. Helping others will be part of your process, which will bring excellent benefits.

Improving your luck

Self-sacrifice, along with discipline and personal discrimination, bring luck. Don't let people use you because this will only result in more emotional baggage. The law of karma states that what you give, you will receive in greater measure; but sometimes the more you give, the more people take, too. Remember that.

The 1st, 8th, 15th and 20th hours of Tuesdays will be lucky times this year.

Try the numbers 7, 16, 25 and 34 to increase your luck.

8 is the year of Saturn

Overview

The number 8 is the most practical of the numbers, being ruled by Saturn and Capricorn. This means that your discipline, attention to detail and hard work will help you achieve your goals. Remaining solitary and not being overly involved with people will help you focus on things that matter. Resisting temptation will be part of your challenge this year, but doing so will also help you become a better person.

Love and pleasure

Balance your personal affairs with work. If you pay too much attention to your work, finances and your professional esteem, you may be missing out on the simple things in life, mainly love and affection.

Being responsible is certainly a great way to show your love to the ones who matter to you, such as your family members. But if you're concerned only with work and no play, it makes for a very dull family life. Make a little more time to enjoy your family and friends and schedule some time off on the weekends so you can enjoy the journey, not just the goal.

LEO

Work

You can make a lot of money this year and, if you've been focused on your work for the last couple of years, this is a time when money should flow to you. The Chinese believe the number 8 is indeed the money number and can bring you the fruits of your hard labour.

Because you're cautious and resourceful you'll be able to save more this year, but try not to be too stingy with your money.

Under an 8 year you'll take on new responsibilities. You mustn't do this for the sake of looking good. If you truly like the work that is being offered, by all means take it. But if it's simply for the sake of ego, you'll be very disappointed.

Improving your luck

This year you could be a little reluctant to try new things. But if you are overly cautious, you may miss opportunities. Don't act impulsively on what is being offered, of course, but do be open to trying some alternative things as well.

Be gentle and kind to yourself. By pampering yourself you send out a strong signal to the universe that you are deserving of some rewards.

The 1st, 8th, 15th and 20th hours of Saturdays are the best times for you in 2011.

The numbers 1, 8, 17, 26 and 35 are your lucky numbers.

9 is the year of Mars

Overview

The year 2011 is the final year of a nine-year cycle and this will be dominated by Aries and Mars. You'll be rushing madly to complete many things, so be careful not to overstep the mark of your capability. Work hard but balance your life with adequate rest.

In your relationships you will realise that you are at odds with your partner and want different things. This is the time to talk it out. If the communication between you isn't flowing well, you might find yourself leaving the relationship and moving on to bigger or better things. Worthwhile communication is a two-way street that will benefit both of you.

Love and pleasure

Mars is very pushy and infuses the number 9 with this kind of energy. The upshot is you need to be gentle in conveying your ideas and offering your views. Avoid arguments if you want to improve your relationships.

If you feel it's time for a change, discuss it with your partner. You can work through this feeling together and create an exciting new pathway for your love life. Don't get too angry with the little things in life. Get out and play some sport if you feel you are inappropriately taking out your bad moods on the ones you love.

LEO

Work

You have an intense drive and strong capability to achieve anything you choose in 2011. But be careful you don't overdo things, because you are prone to pushing yourself too far. Pace your deadlines, stagger the workload and, if possible, delegate some of the more menial tasks to others so you'll have time to do your own work properly.

Number 9 has an element of leadership associated with it, so you may be asked to take over and lead the group. This brings with it added responsibility but can also inspire you greatly.

Improving your luck

Restlessness is one of the problems that the number 9 brings with it, so you must learn to meditate and pacify your mind so you can take advantage of what the universe has to offer. If you're scattered in your energies, your attention will miss vital opportunities and your relationships could also become rather problematic as well.

Your health and vitality will remain strong as long as you rest adequately and find suitable outlets for your tension.

The 1st, 8th, 15th and 20th hours of Tuesdays will be lucky for you throughout 2011. Your lucky numbers are 9, 18, 27 and 36.

LEO

2011:
Your Daily Planner

> *I love life because what more is there*
>
> —Anthony Hopkins

There is a little-known branch of astrology called electional astrology, and it can help you select the most appropriate times for many of your day-to-day activities.

Ancient astrologers understood the planetary patterns and how they impacted on each of us. This allowed them to suggest the best possible times to start various important activities. Many farmers today still use this approach: they understand the phases of the Moon, and attest to the fact that planting seeds on certain lunar days produces a far better crop than planting on other days.

The following section covers many areas of day-to-day life, and uses the cycles of the Moon and the combined strength of the other planets to work out the best times to start different types of activity.

So to create your own personal almanac, first select the activity you are interested in, then quickly scan the year for the best months to start it. When you have selected the month, you can finetune your timing by finding the best specific dates. You can then be sure that the planetary energies will be in sync with you, offering you the best possible outcome.

Coupled with what you know about your monthly and weekly trends, the daily planner can be a powerful tool to help you capitalise on opportunities that come your way this year.

Good luck, and may the planets bless you with great success, fortune and happiness in 2011!

Starting activities

How many times have you made a new year's resolution to begin a diet or be a better person in your relationships? And how many times has it not worked out? Well, part of the reason may be that you started out at the wrong time, because how successful you are is strongly influenced by the position of the Moon and the planets when you begin a particular activity. You will be more successful with the following endeavours if you start them on the days indicated.

Relationships

We all feel more empowered on some days than on others. This is because the planets have some power over us—their movement and their relationships to each other determine the ebb and flow of our energies. And our level of self-confidence and our sense of romantic magnetism play an important part in the way we behave in relationships.

Your daily planner tells you the ideal dates for meeting new friends, initiating a love affair, spending time with family and loved ones—it even tells you the most appropriate times for sexual encounters.

You'll be surprised at how much more impact you can make in your relationships when you tune yourself in to the planetary energies on these special dates.

Falling in love or restoring love

During these times you could expect favourable energies to be present to meet your soulmate. Or, if you've had difficulty in a relationship, you can approach the one you love to rekindle both your and their emotional responses.

January	8, 9, 10, 13, 14, 15, 18, 19, 20, 21
February	4, 5, 6, 9, 10, 11, 14
March	1, 9, 10, 14, 15, 16, 17
April	5, 6, 17, 25, 26
May	3, 4, 6, 7, 8, 9, 10, 11, 14, 15, 22, 23, 24
June	1, 11, 18, 19, 20, 28, 29, 30
July	7, 8, 26, 27, 30, 31
August	3, 12, 13, 14, 22, 23, 27, 31
September	1, 18, 19, 20, 26, 27, 28, 29, 30
October	12, 13, 17, 18, 25, 26, 29, 30, 31
November	2, 3, 4, 5, 6, 9, 17, 29
December	3, 7, 8, 11, 14, 15, 18, 19, 29, 30

Special times with friends and family

Socialising, partying and having a good time with those you enjoy being with is highly favourable under the following dates. These are also excellent days to spend time with family and loved ones in a domestic environment:

LEO

January	17, 20, 21
February	2, 9, 10, 11, 18, 19, 20, 21, 22, 23, 24, 28
March	1, 11, 14, 16, 17, 20
April	2, 11, 12, 21, 22, 26
May	6, 9, 10, 11, 14, 15, 22, 23, 24
June	4, 8, 10, 12, 19, 20, 25, 26, 28
July	7, 8, 16, 23, 30, 31
August	4, 5, 6, 7, 13, 20, 27, 31
September	1, 6, 18, 19, 20, 29, 30
October	1, 16, 17, 25, 26
November	2, 12, 13, 17, 26, 29
December	11, 14, 15, 18, 19, 27, 28

Healing or resuming a relationship

If you're trying to get back together with the one you love and need a heart-to-heart or deep and meaningful conversation, you can try the following dates to do so:

January	2, 3, 4, 5, 6, 7, 8, 9, 10, 11, 12, 13, 14, 15, 16, 17, 18, 19, 20, 21, 28
February	1, 2, 4, 5, 6, 7, 21, 22, 23, 24, 28
March	1, 8, 9, 10, 11, 14, 16, 17, 18, 19, 20
April	2, 11, 12, 26

2011: YOUR DAILY PLANNER

May	1, 6, 7, 8, 9, 10, 11, 12, 13, 15, 19, 22, 24, 25, 26, 27, 28
June	5, 12, 14, 15, 16, 19, 23, 25, 26, 27, 28, 29, 30
July	4, 6, 7, 8, 9, 10, 16, 19, 21, 23, 28, 29, 30, 31
August	1, 2, 3, 13, 15, 16, 20, 27, 29, 30, 31
September	1, 2, 3, 4, 5, 6, 13, 15, 16, 17, 18, 19, 20, 21, 22, 23, 25, 28, 29
October	12, 13, 15, 16, 17, 18, 25, 27, 29
November	2, 4, 5, 6, 15, 16, 17, 26, 29
December	11, 19, 20, 21, 22, 23

Sexual encounters

Physical and sexual energies are well favoured on the following dates. The energies of the planets enhance your moments of intimacy during these times:

January	2, 3, 4, 5, 6, 7, 8, 9, 10, 11, 12, 20, 21, 25
February	7, 8, 18, 19, 20, 21
March	1, 8, 11, 14, 20, 21
April	4, 11, 12, 25, 26, 27, 28, 29
May	2, 9, 10, 11, 14, 15, 22, 23, 24
June	1, 11, 12, 18, 19, 20, 28, 29, 30

LEO

July	7, 8, 16, 19, 20, 21, 23, 30
August	3, 12, 13, 14, 20, 22, 27, 31
September	1, 18, 19, 20, 29, 30
October	1, 13, 15, 18, 19, 20, 21, 22, 25, 26
November	2, 3, 11, 15, 16, 17, 18, 21, 22
December	5, 6, 12, 13, 14, 15, 18, 19

Health and wellbeing

Your aura and life force are susceptible to the movements of the planets; in particular, they respond to the phases of the Moon.

The following dates are the most appropriate times to begin a diet, have cosmetic surgery, or seek medical advice. They also tell you when the best times are to help others.

Feeling of wellbeing

Your physical as well as your mental alertness should be strong on these following dates. You can plan your activities and expect a good response from others:

January	7, 9, 10, 11, 12, 13, 14, 18, 20, 21
February	4, 18, 19, 20, 21, 22, 23, 24
March	16, 17, 19, 20
April	2, 7, 12, 20, 22, 25, 26
May	9, 10, 11, 14, 15, 16, 17, 22, 24, 25

2011: YOUR DAILY PLANNER

June	4, 8, 10, 11, 12, 16, 17, 18, 19, 20, 21, 23, 25, 26
July	7, 8, 9, 10, 26, 27, 30
August	3, 4, 5, 6, 12, 13, 14, 17, 19, 22, 27, 31
September	1, 13, 26, 27, 28, 29, 30
October	1, 16, 17, 25, 26, 30, 31
November	1, 2, 3, 4, 5, 6, 17, 29
December	4, 11, 14, 15, 18, 19, 21, 22, 23, 30

Healing and medical

These times are good for approaching others who have expertise when you need some deeper understanding. They are also favourable for any sort of healing or medication, and for making appointments with doctors or psychologists. Planning surgery around these dates should bring good results.

Often giving up our time and energy to assist others doesn't necessarily result in the expected outcome. By lending a helping hand to a friend on the following dates, the results should be favourable.

January	1, 2, 3, 4, 5, 6, 7, 8, 14, 15, 16, 17, 18, 19, 20, 21, 22, 23, 24, 25, 26, 27, 28, 29, 31
February	3, 4, 5, 6, 7, 8, 9, 10, 13, 15, 16, 17, 18, 19, 21, 22, 23, 24, 25, 26, 27
March	4, 9, 10, 11, 12, 15, 16

April	2, 9, 10, 11, 12, 13, 14, 15, 16, 17, 18, 19, 20, 21, 22, 23, 24, 25, 26, 27, 28, 29, 30
May	1, 2, 3, 4, 5, 6, 8, 9, 10, 11, 12, 13, 14, 15, 16, 17, 18, 19, 20, 21, 22, 23, 24, 25, 30
June	23, 26, 28
July	3, 10, 11, 12
August	7, 8, 9, 10, 11, 12, 13, 14, 15, 16, 20, 21, 25
September	23, 25, 26, 27
October	20, 21, 22, 23, 24, 25, 26, 27, 28, 29, 30, 31
November	1, 2, 3, 4, 5, 6, 7, 8, 9, 10, 11, 12, 13, 14, 15, 16, 17, 18, 19, 20, 21, 22, 23, 24, 25, 30
December	1, 2, 3, 4, 5, 6, 7, 8, 9, 10, 30

Money

Money is an important part of life, and involves lots of decisions—decisions about borrowing, investing, spending. The ideal times for transactions are very much influenced by the planets, and whether your investment or nest egg grows or doesn't grow can often be linked to timing. Making your decisions on the following dates could give you a whole new perspective on your financial future:

Managing wealth and money

To build your nest egg it's a good time to open a bank account and invest money on the following dates:

January	2, 3, 9, 10, 11, 12, 13, 14, 15, 16, 17, 18, 19, 20, 21, 22, 24, 28
February	3, 4, 5, 6, 7, 8, 9, 11, 13, 14, 16, 18, 19, 20, 21, 22, 23, 24, 25, 26, 27
March	4, 8, 11, 12, 13, 14, 16, 17, 18, 19
April	2, 7, 8, 9, 10, 11, 12, 13, 16, 17, 18, 19, 20, 21, 22, 23, 24, 25
May	1, 6, 7, 8, 9, 10, 11, 12, 13, 14, 15, 16, 17, 18, 19, 20, 21, 22, 23, 24, 25, 30
June	3, 4, 5, 8, 16, 17, 18, 19, 20, 23, 25, 26, 27, 28
July	4, 5, 6, 7, 8, 9, 10, 11, 12, 16, 23, 25, 28, 29, 30, 31
August	1, 2, 3, 4, 5, 6, 7, 8, 9, 10, 11, 12, 13, 14, 15, 16, 17, 19, 20, 30, 31
September	2, 11, 13, 15, 23, 25, 26, 27, 28, 29, 30
October	1, 2, 3, 4, 5, 6, 7, 8, 13, 14, 15, 16, 17, 18, 19, 21, 24, 25, 26, 27, 28, 29, 30, 31
November	2, 3, 4, 5, 6, 7, 9, 11, 12, 13, 14, 15, 16, 17, 18, 19, 20, 23, 25, 29
December	6, 13, 19, 26, 31

LEO

Spending

It's always fun to spend, but the following dates are more in tune with this activity and are likely to give you better results:

January	8, 9, 10, 11, 12, 13, 14, 15
February	9, 11, 18, 19
March	9
April	22
May	6, 7, 8, 9, 10, 11, 12, 13, 14, 17, 18, 19, 20, 21, 22, 23, 24
June	4, 8, 10, 11, 12, 14, 16, 17, 19
July	6, 7, 8, 9, 10, 11, 31
August	1, 2, 3, 4, 5, 6, 15, 16, 17, 18, 19, 30, 31
September	1, 2, 3, 4, 17, 19, 28, 29, 30
October	12, 13, 14, 15, 16, 17, 18, 19, 27, 28, 29, 30, 31
November	2, 3, 4, 5, 6, 7
December	3, 4, 5, 22, 23

Selling

If you're thinking of selling something, whether it is small or large, consider the following dates as ideal times to do so:

2011: YOUR DAILY PLANNER

January	2, 3, 9, 10, 11, 12, 13, 14, 15, 16, 17, 18, 19, 20, 22, 24, 28
February	3, 4, 5, 6, 7, 8, 9, 11, 13, 14, 16, 18, 19, 20, 21, 22, 23, 24, 25, 26, 27
March	4, 8, 11, 12, 13, 14, 16, 17, 18, 19
April	2, 7, 8, 9, 10, 11, 12, 13, 16, 17, 18, 19, 20, 21, 22, 23, 24
May	1, 6, 7, 8, 9, 10, 11, 12, 13, 14, 15, 16, 17, 18, 19, 20, 21, 22, 23, 24, 25, 26, 30
June	3, 4, 5, 8, 16, 17, 18, 19, 20, 23, 25, 26, 27, 28
July	4, 5, 6, 7, 8, 9, 10, 11, 12, 16, 23, 25, 28, 29, 30, 31
August	1, 2, 3, 4, 5, 6, 7, 8, 9, 10, 11, 12, 13, 14, 15, 16, 17, 19, 20, 30, 31
September	2, 11, 13, 15, 23, 25, 26, 27, 28, 29, 30
October	1, 2, 3, 4, 5, 6, 7, 8, 13, 14, 15, 16, 17, 18, 19, 21, 24, 25, 26, 27, 28, 29, 30, 31
November	2, 3, 4, 5, 6, 7, 9, 11, 12, 13, 14, 15, 16, 17, 18, 19, 20, 23, 25, 29
December	2, 3, 4, 5, 6, 7, 11, 30

Borrowing

Few of us like to borrow money, but if you must, taking out a loan on the following dates will be positive:

LEO

January	1, 20, 21, 26, 27, 28, 31
February	1, 2, 22, 23, 24
March	1, 22, 23, 26, 27, 29, 31
April	1, 18, 19, 22, 23, 24, 25, 26, 27, 28, 29
May	17, 18, 19, 20, 21, 22, 23, 24, 25, 26
June	16, 17, 18, 19, 22
July	15, 16, 28, 29, 30
August	15, 16, 24, 25, 26, 27, 28
September	21, 22
October	21
November	14, 15, 16, 17, 23, 24
December	12, 13, 14, 15, 20, 21, 22, 23, 24

Speculation and investment

To invest your money and get a good return on that investment try taking a punt on the following dates:

January	3, 4, 5, 11, 12, 18, 19, 24, 25, 31
February	1, 7, 8, 14, 15, 20, 21, 27, 28
March	6, 7, 8, 14, 15, 20, 21, 26, 27
April	2, 3, 4, 10, 11, 16, 17, 22, 23, 24, 30
May	1, 7, 8, 14, 15, 20, 21, 27, 28, 29
June	3, 4, 5, 10, 11, 16, 17, 23, 24, 25
July	1, 2, 7, 8, 14, 15, 21, 22, 28, 29

August	3, 4, 10, 11, 17, 18, 19, 24, 25, 26, 31
September	1, 6, 7, 13, 14, 15, 21, 22, 27, 28
October	3, 4, 5, 11, 12, 18, 19, 25, 26, 31
November	1, 7, 8, 14, 15, 16, 21, 22, 27, 28
December	4, 5, 6, 12, 13, 18, 19, 25, 26, 31

Work and education

Your career is important to you, and continual improvement of your skills is therefore also crucial, professionally, mentally and socially. These dates will help you find out the most appropriate times to improve your professional talents and commence new work or education associated with your work.

You may need to decide when to start learning a new skill, when to ask for a promotion, and even when to make an important career change. Here are the days when your mental and educational power is strong.

Learning new skills

Educational pursuits are lucky and bring good results on the following dates:

January	16, 17
February	12, 13
March	11, 12, 13, 18, 19
April	7, 8, 9, 14, 15
May	5, 6, 12, 13

LEO

June	2, 8, 9, 14, 15
July	5, 6, 11, 12, 13
August	1, 2, 8, 9, 29, 30
September	4, 5
October	1, 2, 29, 30
November	25, 26
December	9, 10

Changing career path or profession

If you're feeling stuck and need to move into a new professional activity, changing jobs is recommended at these times:

January	4, 5, 13, 14, 15
February	9, 10, 11
March	1, 2, 3, 9, 10, 11, 12, 18, 19, 20, 21
April	5, 6, 7, 8, 9, 14, 15, 16, 17, 25, 26
May	3, 4, 12, 13, 22, 23, 24
June	1, 2, 8, 9, 18, 19, 20, 28, 29, 30
July	5, 6, 14, 26, 27
August	3, 4, 10, 11, 22, 23, 29, 30, 31
September	1, 6, 7, 8, 9, 10, 18, 19, 20, 27, 28
October	3, 4, 5, 16, 17, 25, 26, 31
November	1, 2, 3, 9, 10, 29, 30
December	1, 7, 8, 9, 10, 11, 18, 19, 25, 26, 27, 28

Promotion, professional focus and hard work

To increase your mental focus and achieve good results from the work you do; promotions are also likely on the dates that follow:

January	3, 9, 10, 11, 12, 13, 14, 18
February	22, 23, 24, 25, 26, 27, 28
March	8, 10, 11, 13, 14, 16, 17, 18, 19
April	11, 12
May	6, 7, 8, 9, 10, 11, 12, 13, 15, 16, 17, 19, 21, 22, 23, 24
June	4, 5, 8, 11, 12, 14, 15, 16, 17, 19
July	16, 18, 19, 20, 23, 24, 25, 28, 29, 30
August	1, 2, 14, 15, 16, 17, 19, 30
September	1, 2, 3, 4, 5, 6, 11, 13, 16, 17, 19
October	13, 15, 16, 17, 18, 19
November	2, 4, 5, 6, 7, 12
December	25, 26

Travel

Setting out on a holiday or adventurous journey is exciting. Here are the most favourable times for doing this. Travel on the following dates is likely to give you a sense of fulfilment:

January	9, 10, 11, 12, 16, 17, 18, 19
February	4, 5, 6, 7, 15
March	19

LEO

April	7, 8, 9, 10, 11
May	15
June	4, 8, 10, 11
July	1, 5, 6
August	1, 2, 3, 4, 8
September	27, 28
October	1, 3, 4, 29, 30, 31
November	1, 4, 5, 6
December	3, 4, 5, 25, 29, 30

Beauty and grooming

Believe it or not, cutting your hair or nails has a powerful effect on your body's electromagnetic energy. If you cut your hair or nails at the wrong time of the month, you can reduce your level of vitality significantly. Use these dates to ensure you optimise your energy levels by staying in tune with the stars:

Haircuts

January	1, 2, 8, 9, 10, 16, 17, 28, 29, 30
February	25, 26
March	4, 5, 11, 12, 13, 14, 25, 31
April	1, 7, 8, 9, 20, 21, 27, 28, 29
May	5, 6, 18, 19, 25, 26
June	1, 2, 14, 15, 21, 22, 28, 29, 30
July	11, 12, 13, 18, 19, 20, 26, 27

August	8, 9, 15, 16, 22, 23
September	4, 5, 11, 12, 18, 19, 20
October	1, 2, 8, 9, 10, 16, 17, 29, 30
November	4, 5, 6, 12, 13, 25, 26
December	2, 3, 9, 10, 11, 23, 24, 29, 30

Therapies, massage and self-pampering

January	1, 2, 8, 9, 10, 16, 17, 28, 29, 30
February	5, 6, 12, 13, 25, 26
March	4, 5, 11, 12, 13, 24, 25, 31
April	1, 7, 8, 9, 20, 21, 27, 28, 29
May	5, 6, 18, 19, 25, 26
June	1, 2, 14, 15, 21, 22, 28, 29, 30
July	11, 12, 13, 18, 19, 20, 26, 27
August	8, 9, 15, 16, 22, 23
September	4, 5, 11, 12, 18, 19, 20
October	1, 2, 8, 9, 10, 16, 17, 29, 30
November	4, 5, 6, 12, 13, 25, 26
December	2, 3, 9, 10, 11, 23, 24, 29, 30

Discover Pure Reading Pleasure with

MILLS & BOON

Visit the Mills & Boon website for all the latest in romance

- **Buy** all the latest releases, backlist and eBooks
- **Find out** more about our authors and their books
- **Join** our community and chat to authors and other readers
- **Free** online reads from your favourite authors
- **Win** with our fantastic online competitions
- **Sign** up for our free monthly eNewsletter
- **Tell us** what you think by signing up to our reader panel
- **Rate** and review books with our star system

www.millsandboon.co.uk

Follow us at twitter.com/millsandboonuk

Become a fan at facebook.com/romancehq